Public Library of Youngstown and Mahoning Co

30056526514

78 33453

970.3   v.23
American Indian ethnohistory
2083

4-H

THE PUBLIC LIBRARY
of Youngstown and Mahoning County

D1251029

A Garland Series

AMERICAN INDIAN ETHNOHISTORY

Indians of the Southwest

compiled and edited by

DAVID AGEE HORR
Brandeis University

970.3 v. 23

Apache Indians VI

ENVIRONMENT, SETTLEMENT,
AND LAND USE IN THE
JICARILLA APACHE CLAIM AREA

B. L. Gordon, et al.

INDIAN LAND RIGHTS
IN THE JICARILLA APACHE AREA

Donald C. Cutter

PUBLIC LIBRARY
YOUNGSTOWN, OHIO

78 33453

Garland Publishing Inc., New York & London
1974

Copyright© 1974

by Garland Publishing, Inc.

All Rights Reserved

Library of Congress Cataloging in Publication Data

Gordon, Burton Le Roy, 1920-
    Environment, settlement, and land use in the Jicaril-
la Apache claim area.

    (Apache Indians, 6) (American Indian ethnohistory:
Indians of the Southwest)
    1. Jicarilla Indians--Land tenure. I. Cutter,
Donald C. Indian land rights in the Jicarilla Apache
area. 1974. II. Title. III. Series. IV. Series:
American Indian ethnohistory: Indians of the Southwest.
E99.A6A54 no. 6 [E99.J5]   970.3s [333.7'09701]
ISBN 0-8240-0708-5   74-6062

Printed in the United States of America

Contents*

5

*There are twelve volumes on the Apache Indians in the Garland
American Indian Ethnohistory Series. The prefatory material is in
Volume I; the Commission Findings in Volume XII.

**Garland Publishing has repaginated this work (at outside center) to
facilitate scholarly use. However, original pagination has been retained
for internal reference.

LOCATIONS OF
APACHE INDIANS, 1950
(And Original Range)

LEGEND

■ 1950 Location
▨ Original Range

SCALE 1:8,000,000

7

8

ENVIROMENT, SETTLEMENT, AND LAND USE

IN THE JICARILLA APACHE CLAIM AREA

By the Department of Geography,

University of New Mexico

B.L. Gordon, Research Director
Ynez Haase, Research Associate
Edgar G. DeWilde, Research Assistant
Joe W. Hart, Research Assistant

With the collaboration of
Dr. Yi-Fu Tuan, Mr. Philip Vargas,
Mr. Richard Edwards, Mrs.
Judith Bateman, and Mr.
J. G. Widdison.

9

NOTE: This is an abridged and revised version of an
earlier report bearing the same title. The
earlier report concerned the original, larger
claim area.

Claimant's Exhibit No. PLG-1
Docket 22A

Albuquerque: Department of Geography, University of New Mexico
1964

INTRODUCTION

The Jicarilla Apache claim area lies largely in northeastern New Mexico, with a small portion of it extending into Colorado. The extent of the area is about 21,900 square miles, or more than fourteen million acres.

The physical environment of the area is discussed in the first part of this report, since the pattern of land use and the value of the land have been importantly dependent on terrain, climate, plant cover, and soil type. Thereafter is an outline of the economic development of the area and a discussion of its products between 1848 and 1887. American settlement and commerce are described. Particular note has been made of the early recognition of the value of the resources of the area by the United States government.

American settlement was greatly encouraged by United States government land acts. The sites and time of settlement under the land acts is shown in statistical detail in Appendix One.

Furthermore, land value is evidenced by a study of land sales. Deeds of sale of land located by the surveys of the United States General Land Office have been recorded. A map and tabulations in Appendices Two and Three show the location of the land sold, the number of sales, and the average price per acre.

Data in this abridged report were originally gathered for the original, larger claim area. In a few instances, especially in the appendices, it has not been practical to reduce general statements and statistics to the exact confines of the revised claim area. The maps were also drawn for the original area.

12

CONTENTS

Introduction

14

CHAPTER 1

TERRAIN

One of the sharpest physiographic boundaries in the United States is that where the High Plains meet the base of the Rocky Mountains. The Jicarilla Apache claim area lies across this boundary; about a fifth of the area belongs with the Sangre de Cristo range of the Rockies, and the remainder with the flat and rolling surfaces of the High Plains. This is the primary physiographic fact of the claim area.

But the details of relief are much more complex than this basic two-part division suggests. The mountains terminate at the Glorieta Mesa, and southward, to the west of the Pecos Valley, are a few rows of hills and broad basins. The High Plains are also varied. Their slightly undulating expanse is diversified by volcanic peaks, lava-capped mesas, canyons, the winding escarpments of plateaus, and the more occasional sand dunes.

THE MOUNTAINS

The high mountain ranges of the southern Rockies extend through south-central Colorado into north-central New Mexico. Here, east of the Rio Grande, is the Sangre de Cristo Range, the

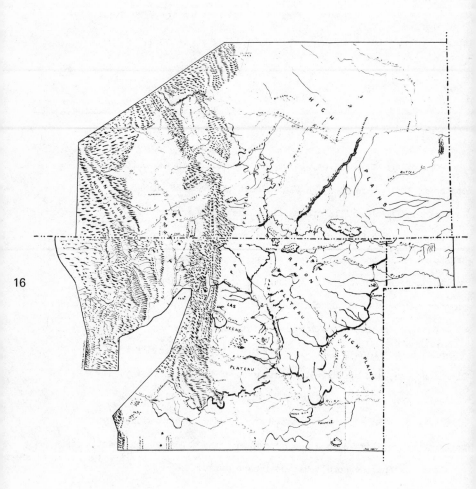

16

dominant relief feature of the claim area. Along its crests and at higher elevations, granite is commonly the surface-forming material; the slopes and foothills are generally formed of sedimentary beds.

That portion of the Sangre de Cristo in the area extends south for about 100 miles from the state line to the headwaters of the Pecos, terminating above Glorieta Mesa. This southern segment of the Sangre de Cristo is the highest and most extensive mountain range in the State of New Mexico. Wheeler Peak, between Taos and Elizabethtown, is the highest point in the state, 13,160 feet above sea level. It is just outside the claim area. Numerous other peaks rise to 10,000 - 13,000 feet above sea level. Near the head of Pecos Canyon, the crest of the mountains divides. The higher and rougher western spur is called the Santa Fe Range; the eastern spur, with broader and more nearly level summits, is called the Las Vegas Range.

17

North of Eagle Nest both the east and west slopes of the Sangre de Cristo are included in the claim area. From Eagle Nest south to Santa Fe Baldy the boundary of the claim area follows the crest or ridge of the mountains -- the east slope only is in the claim area. Southward from Santa Fe Baldy, however, the area includes the considerable width of the Las Vegas Range, and all the headwaters of the Pecos River.

Eagle Nest Lake is located in the Moreno Valley, a high intermontane basin (elev. 9000 feet). Slightly to the west is the main crest of the Sangre de Cristo, while to the east the crest is somewhat lower and is divided into three segments. From north to

south they are the Cimarron Mountains, near the New Mexico-Colorado
line, the Agua Fria Mountains, and the Rincon Mountains. Between
the Cimarron and Agua Fria Mountains and the main crest of the
Sangre de Cristo lies the Moreno Valley.

Another narrow intermontane basin, the Mora Valley, extends
south of Moreno Valley, between the Sangre de Cristo proper and
the Rincon Range. This valley is drained by the Mora River, a
tributary of the Canadian. It is about fifty miles long and from one-
half to two miles wide. The valley floor slopes southward from
7500 feet at Holman to 6500 feet at Mora. Immediately east of the
lower Mora Valley extend the broad mesas and hills of the Las
Vegas Plateau.

The Sangre de Cristo Mountains are crossed in several places
by rather gentle passes. From north to south, these include:
Red River Pass (9352 feet) and Palo Flechado Pass (9102 feet)
(these two breaks permit entrance from the west into Moreno Valley;
from there passage eastward down out of the mountains is via
Cimarron Canyon); also a pass from the Rio Pueblo to the Mora Valley
(State Road 3), and Glorieta Pass (7432 feet) (Interstate route 25).

A small prt of the San Luis Valley is within the claim area.
This is a high intermontane valley drained by the Rio Grande. But
the claim area includes only that part of it in New Mexico from the
base of the Sangre de Cristo to the river -- north of Arroyo
Hondo and including such other villages as Cerro and Questa. The
elevation is about 8000 feet. This area is sometimes referred to
as Sunshine Valley.

The Rio Grande in the San Luis Valley, where it bounds the claim area, is in a canyon 700 feet deep.

South of the Sangre de Cristo is a hilly area draining into the Galisteo Arroyo, and south from that is the north end of Estancia Valley (or Sandoval Basin). This basin is about sixty-five miles long from north to south, and about forty miles wide, but most of it extends beyond the claim area. The altitude of the valley floor is between 6200 and 6400 feet. The valley has no drainage outlet.

Northeast of Estancia Valley is the dissected south end of Glorieta Mesa, and to the east are the Pedernal Hills, a group of low, quartzitic peaks rising abruptly above the basin surface. Glorieta Mesa is between 7000 and 7600 feet above seal level. The Pedernal Hills reach about the same height.

19

PLATEAUS AND MESAS

East of the Rocky Mountains are the plains. But as noted above, the plains are not a simple physiographic unit; there are numerous topographic breaks. Apart from the canyons, the most prominent break is the Canadian Escarpment, a wall some 500 to 1000 feet high. In New Mexico this escarpment is the boundary between the Plateaus (Las Vegas and Raton Plateaus) and the High Plains. Park Plateau stands above the Las Vegas Plateau in New Mexico, but the escarpment separating them is less pronounced. To further complicate the surface relief of the plateaus, there are numerous volcanic mountains and mesas capped by basaltic lava. This volcanic and mesa topography is especially characteristic of the Raton Plateau. The plateaus and mesas will now be described individually.

Park Plateau--From the latitude of upper Cimarron Creek in extreme northern New Mexico, Park Plateau extends for approximately ninety miles, at elevations of 7000 to 9000 feet, into Colorado. In southern Colorado the plateau rises to 8500 feet on the west side and 7000 to 7500 feet on the east. On the west it is bordered by the Culebra segment of the Sangre de Cristo Mountains and by the Cimarron Range. Eastward the Park Plateau merges with Raton Plateau.

The Raton Plateau--The higher parts of the Raton Plateau are known as the Raton Mesas. Most of them are capped by lava.

20

> The Raton mesas are all true table-lands, having flat tops and precipitous slopes on all sides. The surface from which they rise is a part of the Great Plains, which at the western end of the mesas region is about a

> mile above sea level. This surface falls
> gently away from the mesas to the south,
> east, and north; and the streams rising in
> these highlands radiate from them in these
> three directions, winding over the mile-
> high plain for considerable distances before
> dropping into the narrow canyons, some of
> which are more than 1000 feet deep (Lee,
> 1921, p. 384).

More commonly, however, the name Raton Mesa refers only to the tableland north of Raton, the highest and best known of the four principal mesas of the plateau. Numerous volcanic peaks and craters are scattered over the area south of the mesas.

The Raton Mesa includes most of the area between Trinidad and Raton. Part of its surface rises above the 9000 foot contour line. At its north end is Fishers Peak (9586 feet), some 3600 feet above, and overlooking Trinidad. Northeast of Trinidad, the Plateau country gives way to the High Plains.

21

Bartlett Mesa covers approximately the same total area as Raton Mesa, but is from 500 to 1000 feet lower; its bounding scarps are extremely steep.

Near the northwest edge of Bartlett Mesa is Raton Pass (7800 feet), a narrow north-south defile, the dividing line between the Raton and the Park Plateaus. The pass is also the water divide between the Arkansas River and the Canadian River.

Six miles east of the city of Raton rises Johnson Mesa, some eleven miles long and six miles wide. Its

average elevation is approximately 8500 feet above the
sea. To the east of the mesa is the cone of Towndrow
Peak and several other volcanic peaks.

The easternmost and most extensive of the four
principal mesas of the Raton Plateau is the Mesa de Maya,
to the north of the Colorado-New Mexico line. It has its
greatest extent, about twenty-four miles, from northwest
to southeast and is from six to eight miles wide. The
average elevation is about 6500 feet, some 500 to 1000
feet above adjacent valleys and plains.

East of Johnson Mesa and south of Mesa de Maya at
the headwaters of the Dry Cimarron and North Canadian
rivers is a lower-lying much dissected region. Low hills,
mesas, buttes, and rugged cliffs are characteristic. East
of Johnson Mesa, near Folsom, is Emery Peak (7350 feet),
separated from Devoy's Peak (6740 feet) by the headwaters
of the Dry Cimarron. Another table-land, Black Mesa,
stands at the boundary between New Mexico, Colorado, and
Oklahoma.

From its source near Johnson Mesa, the Dry Cimarron
flows eastward in a winding canyon along the Colorado-
New Mexico line and enters the Oklahoma Panhandle. Here
the rough mesa and hill country gives way to knolls and
rolling plains.

South of Raton, Bartlett, and Johnson mesas, there
are four conspicuous volcanic peaks along a line extending
eastward from Canadian River. Eagle Tail Peak (ca. 7800

feet), the most westerly; Laughlin Peak (8836 feet);
Mount Capulin (ca. 8700 feet), a nearly symmetrical cinder
cone which rises more than 1200 feet above lava flows on
which it rests; Sierra Grande (8732 feet), easternmost
of the group.

South of these volcanic peaks, elevations decrease
gradually to a broad, gently undulating surface developed
over sandstones and shales. This surface terminates at
the edge of the Canadian Escarpment which overlooks the
High Plains.

Las Vegas Plateau--This high surface lies below, and
south of Park Plateau, west of the canyon of the Canadian
River and north of the Canadian Escarpment. Its western
boundary is the front of the Sangre de Cristo Mountains
and the high Ocate Mesa. Most of the Las Vegas Plateau
consists of a grass-covered, gently rolling surface cut
in nearly horizontal sedimentary rocks.

23

A few islands stand above the general level of the
plateau. Two of the most prominent ones occur on either
side of the village of Wagon Mound. The higher one to
the west, the Turkey Mountains, stands 1800 feet above
the plateau surface. They are carved mostly out of
sedimentary rocks. On the east, 800 feet above the
surrounding country, are the Cornudo Hills, capped by
lava.

The Ocate Mesa extends from the base of the Sangre
de Cristo Mountains to the Las Vegas Plateau. It is

made up of lava sheets, some of which probably came from
the Ocate Crater (8902 feet) at the south end of the Mesa.
Its surface elevation exceeds 8200 feet above sea level,
which makes it comparable to the Bartlett and Johnson
mesas farther north.

THE HIGH PLAINS

Beyond the high plateaus and mesas are the plains.
These slighty corrugated surfaces occupy the greater
part of eastern Colorado and New Mexico, and slope
imperceptibly eastward. At the northern edge of Raton
Plateau elevation is about 9000 feet; but at the southern
edge of the plateau, elevation falls from 6000 feet to less
than 3800 feet in the lower Canadian Valley, northeast of
Tucumcari.

South of Trinidad the line dividing the plateaus from
the plains swings abruptly eastward around the Mesa de Maya,
then again turns southward and westward, where it continues
as the Canadian Escarpment. North of the Canadian River
Valley, these plains out eastward from the escarpment are
known as the High Plains; south of the valley, they are
called the Llano Estacado or Staked Plain, a name given, it
is said, by early travelers who found the area so featureless
as to require their driving stakes to mark their course.
Only the northernmost edges of the Llano Estacado are included
in the claim area.

The plains are rolling, and in some places almost
flat. Still there are a few features rising above the

general level. Perhaps the most conspicuous toptgraphic
feature is Rabit Ear Mountain (5940 feet), several miles
north of Clayton, New Mexico. Mesa Rica or Carpenter Mesa
west of Tucumcari is a detached table-land of the Raton
Plateau. It has an elevation of 4765 feet, about 750 feet
above the Canadian River, which flows along its south base.
A landmark twelve miles south of Tucumcari is flat-topped
Mesa Redondo, which rises about 800 feet above the surrounding surface.

DRAINAGE

A brief survey of the drainage system allows one to
gain insight into the major routes in and out of the claim
area, and into possibilities of land use. The major drainage lines are eastward across the High Plains (the Dry
Cimarron and Canadian Rivers), and southeast (the Pecos River).
The major rivers of this area have cut canyons. This
entrenchment occurs not only in their mountainous headstream
areas, which is to be expected, but also on nearly level
plateaus.

The Pecos River rises within the claim area, in the
southern part of the Sangre de Cristo Mountains. Its
southward course in the mountains is deflected southeast-
ward along the northern scarp of Glorieta Mesa. This
passageway, scooped out by the Pecos River, is the easiest
line of communication between Santa Fe and Las Vegas.
Leaving the mountains and the mesa, the Pecos has cut some
50 feet into the surface. This entrenchment, though not

25

necessarily of the dimensions of a "canyon", is characteristic of many of the larger rivers in the claim area. It is true that some of the deepened floors may be fairly wide, yet it remains a fact that entrenchment has diminished possibilities of irrigation and land use. The Canadian River, the other major river of the High Plains and plateaus, is similarly trenched into a resistant sandstone-capped surface. North of the Canadian escarpment the Canadian Canyon is about 1,000 feet deep. Two headstreams of the Canadian River, Cimarron Creek and Mora River cut across the crest of the front range of the Sangre de Cristo Mountains, and portions of their upper courses lie in the longitudinal intermontane valleys west of the first line of mountains rising above the plateau.

26

The Dry Cimarron is only the largest of several watercourses draining the plains eastward in the area northeast of the Canadain River. These streams, such as Corrumpa and Carrizo Creeks, have no mountain headwaters. They therefore have little water at all.

Literature Cited

Fenneman, Nevin M. _Physiography of Western United States._
     New York: 1931, 534 pp.

Hayden, Ferdinand V. "Report of Agricultural Capacity
     of the Rocky Mountain Region," _Geological Survey of_
     the Territories. Washington: 1869.

Lee, Willis T, "The Raton Mesas of New Mexico and
     Colorado," _The Geographical Review,_ XI (1921),
     pp. 384-397.

United States Geological Survey. _Geology and Water_
     Resources of Estancia Valley, New Mexico, by
     Oscar E. Meinzer, Water Supply Paper 275. Washington
     1911. '98 pp.

Literature Consulted   27

Bowman, Isaiah. _Forest Physiography._ New York: 1911.
     759 pp.

Brown, Ralph H. _Historical Geography of the United States._
     New York: 1948. 596 pp.

Fenneman, Nevin M. "Physiographic Boundaries within the
     United States," _Annals of the Association of American_
     Geographers, IV (1914), pp. 84-98.

Hill, Robert T. "Notes on the Texas-New Mexican Region,
     Bulletin of the Geological Society of America, III
     (1892), pp. 85-100.

Montgomery, Arthur, and Patrick K. Sutherland. _Trail Guide to the_
     Upper Pecos. Socorro: State Bureau of Mines and Mineral
     Resources, 1960.

Philmont Country. U. S. Geological Survey, Professional Paper, 1964.

Lobeck, Armin K. <u>Physiographic Diagram of the United</u>
<u>States</u>. New York: 1922. 8pp.

Miller, Joseph. <u>New Mexico</u>. New York: 1953. 471 pp.

United States Department of Agriculture. <u>Watershed</u>
<u>Resources and Problems of the Upper Rio Grande Basin</u>.
by Edward J. Dortignac. Forest Service Publication.
Fort Collins: September, 1956. 107pp.

_____. <u>Guidebook of the</u>
<u>Western United States: Part C. The Santa Fe Route</u>.
<u>with a side Trip to the Grand Canyon of the Colorado</u>.
by N. H. Darton and others. Bulletin 613.
Washington: 1915. 194 pp.

United States Geological Survey. <u>Physiography and</u>
<u>Quaternary Geology of the San Juan Mountains</u>.
<u>Colorado</u>, by W. W. Atwood and K. F. Mather.
Professional Paper 166. Washington: 1932. 176 pp.

_____. <u>A Gazetteer of Colorado</u>.
by Henry Gannett. Bulletin 291. Washington:
1906. 185 pp.

_____. <u>The Ore Deposits of</u>
<u>New Mexico</u>, by Waldeman, Lindgren and others.
Professional Paper 68. Washington: 1910.
361 pp.

Upson, J. E. "Physiographic Subdivisions of the San
Luis Valley, Southern Colorado," The Journal of
Geology, XLVII (January-December, 1939) pp. 721-736.

28

Maps Consulted

Army Map Service. Editions of 1958. Scale: 1:250,000.
Printed by the United States Geological Survey.

       <u>Albuquerque Sheet</u>, NI 13-1.
       <u>Aztec Sheet</u>, NJ 13-10.
       <u>Dalhart Sheet</u>, NJ 13-2.
       <u>La Junta Sheet</u>, NJ 13-0.
       <u>Raton Sheet</u>, NJ 13-11.
       <u>Santa Fe Sheet</u>, NI 13-2.
       <u>Tucumcari Sheet</u>, NI 13-3.

Lobeck, Armin K. A Physiographic Diagram of the United
    States (Provisional Edition). Chicago: (Not Dated).
    Scale: 1:3,000,000.

Raisz, Erwin J. Map of the Landforms of the United
    States to accompany Atwood's Physiographic Provinces
    of North America. Cambridge: 1939. Scale: one and
    one-eighth inch equals 200 miles.

United States Geological Survey. Scale: 1:5,000,000.

            Colorado (Topographic, 1956)
            New Mexico (Topographic, provisional, 1955)

29

30

CHAPTER 2

CLIMATE

From the viewpoint of land use, the most important
climatic elements are temperature, including length of
growing season, and precipitation. Winds will be
described in their relationship to temperature and
rainfall.

TEMPERATURE AND GROWING SEASON

Climate is closely related to topography; not only
to elevation but to the shape, direction and arrangement
of mountains and valleys. The western part of the claim
area is mountainous, with high intermontane valleys.
Its climatic pattern is therefore much more complex than
that of the plateaus and plains to the east.

Taking first the simpler, eastern part of the claim
area, the following characteristics of temperature may
be noted. In summer, average temperature decreases very
gradually poleward; from about 80°F. in the Tucumcari area to
the high mesas of Raton Plateau, where average July
temperature descends to less than 70°F. In winter,
temperatures are again highest in the south, in the
Tucumcari area (average temperature: 38°F.). And again

the lowest temperature corresponds to the higher parts of the Raton and Park plateaus.

The average length of growing season in the eastern part of the claim area shows a pattern similar to temperature. The number of days between the first and last killing frost drops from 180-200 days at the southern edge to less than 160 days northward. However, an important point to remember when considering these average figures is unseasonal weather caused by waves of unimpeded arctic air from the northwest.

Within the Sangre de Cristo mountain part of the claim area, the three physiographic types of mountains, foothills and high valleys display each a distinctive temperature regime.

32

Mountains--The mountains have the most variable climate. The prevailing winds are from the west, and on exposed summits and passes may blow with great force, in contrast to pockets of calm in the sheltered valleys. The strength of the wind makes the air feel colder than it actually is. A noticeable difference in temperature also exists between the lee- and windward flanks of high mountains during daytime in winter. The leeward flanks, where the air descends and is compressed, are often warmer. This warm wind is known as the Chinook. In

early spring it may melt snow and bring unexpectedly
high temperatures to the mountain edge of the High Plains.
But the single most important thermal fact of high
mountains is, of course, its low average temperatures.
Above 9000 feet, frost may be expected every month of
the year (Gittings, p. 808).

Foothills--The foothills, which here may include
the much dissected surface of the Park Plateau, are cool
in summer (65°-70°F.), and mild in winter in comparison
with both the mountains and the high intermontane
valleys. It is distinguished from the mountains and
the open plains to the east in diminished wind movement
and in a narrower temperature range. During cold spells
the mildest weather is found at the mouths of the larger   33
canyons, because local winds there prevent the accumulation
of cold pools of air in the depressions.

Intermontane Valleys--The largest of the inter-
ontane valleys is the San Luis basin and its southward
extension as Taos Valley. Because of its high elevation
(ca. 7500 feet), the summers are cool, with an average
temperature in July of about 62°F. The winters are very
old. The average January temperatures are less than

20°F, and so are even lower than the higher parts of the Park and Raton Plateaus. Minimum temperatures of -40°F. occur, and are the lowest in the claim area. The narrow Moreno Valley in New Mexico shares these characteristics. The growing season of the San Luis basin, a little over 100 days, is much shorter than that of the High Plains (Map 2).

PRECIPITATION

As with temperature, precipitation is closely related to elevation, but directly; the higher the elevation the greater the precipitation (Map 3). This relation is discernible even over the plateaus and plains. Thus most of the plains in the claim area receive 13 to 16 inches of rain a year, but the high mesas of Raton Plateau, and the higher parts of Park Plateau get as much as 20 inches.

Within the Rocky Mountain system, the average annual precipitation varies greatly depending on exposure to moist winds. On exposed mountain slopes precipitation usually exceeds 25 inches a year, much of the water being a contribution from snowfall. The high intermontane valleys, on the other hand, are sheltered from the moist winds, and are remarkably dry. San Luis basin gets less than 8 inches. Thus this small part of the claim area is the driest part in terms of the amount of precipitation; but the consequences of this low precipitation to vegetation and land use are mitigated by a low rate of evaporation in the cool summers, and by contributions from mountain streams.

The summer half of the year yields more precipitation to the claim area than the winter half. This is especially true of the eastern and southern portions of the claim area. In summer, the prevailing winds are from the south. They are moist and unstable, and bring thundery showers to the plains and the southern Rocky Mountains. The region with the greatest number of thunderstorms in the United States is along the Gulf Coast and in the southern Appalachians; but the southern Rocky Mountains form a distinct subsidiary center. Hail may sometimes fall with these showers.

35

Winter precipitation in the western, mountainous part of the claim area is commonly associated with the inflow of polar Pacific air and cyclonic activity (Dorrah, p. 2). The precipitation comes in the form of snow. Again the amount received varies greatly depending on exposure. In some years nearly 300 inches of snow falls on the crest of the Sangre de Cristo, whereas

the adjacent Rio Grande Valley receives little if any.
The heavy snowfall piled into high snowdrifts by strong
winds over the passes affect communications adversely;
but more pertinent perhaps is the fact that the amount
of snowfall and its rate of melt are of great economic
importance along the lower stream courses. Agriculture
in the valleys is largely dependent on irrigation.

36

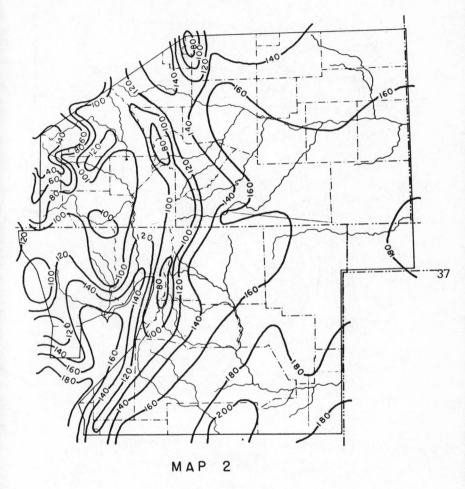

MAP 2

AVERAGE LENGTH OF GROWING SEASON IN DAYS

AFTER: GITTINGS, p. 806 AND HARDY, p. 1022

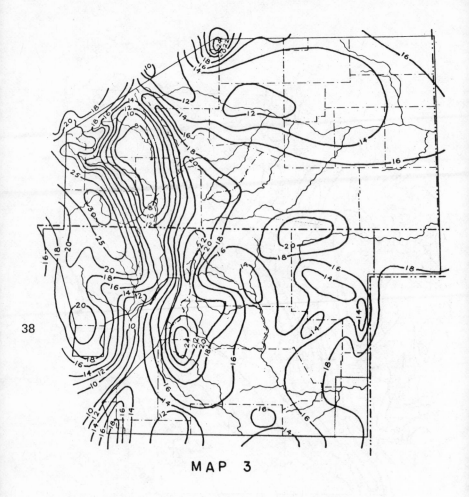

38

MAP 3

AVERAGE ANNUAL PRECIPITATION IN INCHES
AFTER: GITTINGS, p. 807 AND HARDY, p. 1023

Average Dates of Killing Frosts

County	Station	Last in Spring	First in Fall
Colfax	Cimarron	May 6	Oct. 11
	Elizabethtown	June 22	Sept. 9
	Raton	May 9	Oct. 2
	Springer	May 7	Oct. 8
	Vermejo Park	May 25	Sept. 23
Guadalupe	Cuervo	April 12	Nov. 2
	Santa Rosa	April 10	Oct. 27
Harding	Albert	April 17	Oct. 20
	Mosquero	April 26	Oct. 24
	Roy	April 28	Oct. 15
Mora	Ft. Union	May 17	Oct. 5
	Levy	May 8	Oct. 3
	Valmora	May 9	Oct. 11
Quay	Glen Rio	April 10	Oct. 26
	Logan	April 20	Oct. 18
	Montoya	April 3	Nov. 2
San Miguel	Bell Ranch	April 19	Oct. 23
	Las Vegas	May 6	Oct. 8
	Rociado	May 28	Sept. 23
Santa Fe	Stanley	May 14	Oct. 6
Taos	Cerro	May 12	Sept. 30
Torrance	Palma	May 12	Oct. 13
Union	Amistad	April 26	Oct. 24
	Capulin	May 13	Oct. 3
	Clayton	April 23	Oct. 17
Las Animas	Hoehne	May 17	Oct. 6
	Trinidad	May 2	Oct. 16

39

(Hardy, pp. 1011-1024, and
Gittings, pp. 798-808.)

Literature Cited

Dorroh, J.H. "Certain Hydrologic and Climatic
Characteristics of the Southwest," University
of New Mexico Publications in Engineering I
(1946). pp. 1-20.

Gittings, Edwin B. "Climate of Colorado," in Department
of Agriculture, Climate and Man Yearbook of
Agriculture. Washington: 1941. pp. 798,808.

Hardy, Erle L. "Climate of New Mexico" in Department
of Agriculture, Climate and Man, Yearbook
of Agriculture. Washington: 1941. pp.
1011,1024.

Literature Consulted

40

Marvin, Charles F. and Joseph B. Kincer. "Climate,
Temperature, Sunshine, and Wind," in United
States Department of Agriculture, Atlas of
American Agriculture. Washington: 1928.
pp. 1-40.

_____. Climatological Summary, New
Mexico: Precipitation, 1849-1954. State Engineer
Office Technical Report 6. Santa Fe: 1956. 407pp.

Visher, Stephen S. Climatic Atlas of the United States.
Cambridge: 1954. 403pp.

CHAPTER 3

SOILS

The characteristics of a soil depend on a number of soil-forming factors, among them being climate, topography, parent material, vegetation, and time. Therefore it is clear from the complexity of climate and topography in the claim area that the pattern of soils will also be complex. Much less information, however, is available on soils.

GENERAL DESCRIPTION

As with climate and topography, the primary edaphic division in the claim area is between the plains and plateaus in the east and the mountains in the west. In general soils of both provinces are thin, less than 2 feet; on the plains because of low rainfall and low rate of weathering, in the mountains because of steep slopes and rapid erosion. The major difference between them lies in chemical reaction; that of the semi-arid plains is basic, that of the more humid, forested slopes of the mountains (those above 8,000 feet) is neutral or slightly acidic. The soils of the plains belong to the Brown Soil Group and those of the mountains to the Gray Brown Podzolic Group.

BROWN SOIL GROUP OF THE PLAINS. As the name suggests, the soils of the plains show in general a brown color at the surface. The subsoils grade at depths ranging from 1 to 2 feet into light gray or white calcareous layers (Soils and Men, p. 1088). These light-colored soils have evolved in a semi-arid climate under a native vegetation of grasses and shrubs. Their humus content is low compared with the darker colored soils--the Chestnut and Chernozem Groups--east of the claim area in Kansas.

The parent materials are sedimentary beds of clay, shale, and sandstone of varying resistance to weathering. The hard massive sandstones yield but a thin soil, the thinly bedded shales a thicker one. The surface color of the soil also varies from light brown to brown or reddish brown, depending much on the color of the parent materials (Soils and Men, p. 1089). Near Capulin the soils are calcareous loams and clay loams; near Tucumcari, brown non-calcareous granular soils. Subsoils are dominantly calcareous clay.

GRAY_BROWN PODZOLIC GROUP OF THE HIGH MOUNTAINS. In contrast with the lime-rich Brown soils of the plains, the Gray-Brown Podzolic soils of the high mountains have been leached and show an acid chemical reaction. They occur in small pockets in steep, mountainous relief, and extend upward to elevations of 10,000 feet or more, usually to

42

timberline. Above 8,000 feet precipitation is between
25 and 45 inches, much of it as winter snowfall. The
natural vegetation is coniferous forest which yield a
litter of needle leaves to the soil. In the more heavily
forested areas, a gray, leached layer of soil may lie
below the forest litter. Subsoils are generally gray-
brown in color. Only small isolated sites at lower
elevations have been used agriculturally.

In some of the hollows and valley basins at high
elevations, alpine meadows form. These usually have poor
drainage, and may hold small pools of standing water.
Meadow soils are shallow and stony though the top layer
may contain much organic matter, and be dark-brown to
black in color. Soil profiles are but slightly developed.   43

IMMATURE SOILS. There are numerous soil types in
the claim area which do not fall under either of the two
Soil Groups. These have sometimes been referred to as
"immature" soils; that is, soils without well-developed
profiles either because of lack of time or because rapid
erosion on steep slopes has hindered the operation of
soil-forming processes.

Soils on steep slopes do not stay put long enough to
develop profiles. Their characteristics vary with the
parent material and the inclination of the surface. They
are invariably thin and contain much coarse material, and
are hence known as lithosols. The foothills, mesas and

dissected plateaus of the claim area are covered by
complex soils of this type developed from a great
variety of parent materials, including basalt, limestone,
quartzite, sandstone, shale, and outwash material. Thin
and gravelly in texture, the soils range in color from
gray-brown to dark brown. The subsoils are commonly
light gray and calcareous, somewhat cemented; in many
areas, they are exposed through erosion. These soils
are found at elevations of from about 5,400 feet to
around 7000 feet on the east slopes of the Rocky Mountains.

44

SOILS TYPES OF THE CLAIM AREA

NORTHERN PLAINS

NORTHERN PLAINS
(UPLAND SUBDIVISION)

SOUTHERN PLAINS

CENTRAL PLAINS

RIVER ALLUVIUM

MOUNTAINOUS AREA

MESA AND LAVA AREA

SAN LUIS VALLEY

SAND

45

Literature Cited

United States Department of Agriculture. <u>Soils and Men, Yearbook of Agriculture, 1938.</u> 1232pp.

Literature Consulted

Holmes, J. Garnett. "Soil Survey of the San Luis Valley, Colorado, in United States Department of Agriculture, <u>Field Operations of the Bureau of Soils, 1903.</u> (Fifth Report) Washington: 1904. pp. 1099-1119.

46

Marbut, C. F. "Soils of the United States," in United States Department of Agriculture, Atlas of American Agriculture. Washington: 1935. pp. 1-98.

Perry, Ester P. <u>Agricultural Field Report of the Jicarilla Claim Area.</u> Manuscript. Albuquerque: 1959.

United States Department of Agriculture. <u>Irrigation Agriculture in the West.</u> Miscellaneous Publication 670. Washington: 1948. 39pp.

_____. <u>Soils of the San Luis Valley, Colorado,</u> by Macy H. Lapham. Bureau of Chemistry and Soils Circular 52. Washington: 1912. 26pp.

CHAPTER 4

VEGETATION

A traveller in the claim area will readily note
the close correspondence between the plant cover and
terrain, climate, and soil (Natural Vegetation Map).

By far the greater part of the area is grassland,
located especially in the lower and smoother parts.
Coniferous forests, in which pine, spruce and fir are
common trees, are found in the mountainous country where
rainfall is greatest. An open woodland of pinon
and juniper trees is transitional between the grassland
at lower elevations and heavier coniferous forest
upslope. About one percent of the total area
is alpine meadow. Desert shrubs, especially sagebrush
and greasewood, cover about four percent.

At lower elevations, blue grama grass, <u>Bouteloua
gracilis,</u> is the dominant grassland species, with
galleta grass its most widespread associate. In the plains
along the eastern boundary of the area, where the rainfall
is sixteen to eighteen inches per year, "including the
lower Canadian Valley, and in the general vicinity of
Tucumcari, another low grass, namely buffalo grass,
<u>Buchloe dactyloides</u>, enters the association..." (Castetter,
p. 268.) In the drier southeastern parts of the area

"blue grama definitely ranks as the dominant species,
but with it are often found varying amounts of black
grama, Bouteloua eriopoda, especially on sandy and
gravelly soils." (Castetter, p. 268) A Grama-
Muhlenbergia assocdation, of reduced grazing value, appears
under drier conditions at the east base of the Rockies.

Heavy coniferous forest is found at higher elevations,
in areas of increased rainfall. Ponderosa pine, Pinus
ponderosa, generally appears at elevations of 7500 to
8000 feet. Undergrowth beneath ponderosa pine is mainly
grama and other grasses, and low shrubs. In the upper
part of its range, ponderosa pine is mixed with Douglas
fir, Pseudotsuga menziesii, the latter is found upslope
to about 8500 feet. The ponderosa pine-Douglas fir zone
is the most accessible and productive timber producing
area. At around 8500 feet Douglas fir and spruce, Picea
spp., often occur intermixed. The spruce area extends
upslope to the treeline at around 12,000 feet. Included
within this zone, 8500 to 12,000 feet, are fir, Abies
spp., and aspen, Populus tremuloides. The fir stands
are dense at the higher elevations, aspen in the lower
or middle parts of the zone. Especially heavy stands of
aspen cover sites where forest fires and avalanches
have recently occurred. The lavender-flowered New Mexico
locust, Robinia neomexicana, and ferns are also common on

48

such sites, and where there has been heavy logging.

The piñon-juniper association of the open woodland, Pinus edulis and Juniperus monosperma, is found in the foothills and on the lower mountain slopes at elevations of approximately 6400 to 8000 feet on the eastern Rocky Mountains, and at elevations of from 6800 to about 8500 feet around the San Luis valley and westward. Grama and other forage grasses, and low shrubs cover a considerable part of the piñon-juniper zone. And, woody shrubs, for instance, scruboak, Quercus spp. and mountain mahogany, Cercocarpus sp. appear locally in higher parts of the zone, mainly along the east slopes of the Rockies.

The term alpine meadow is often used for tundra-like meadow above climatic timberline. In the claim area such surface is restricted to the higher peaks. As used here, however, the term includes such high altitude grasslands as the Moreno Valley.

These lie below climatic timberline, with heavily forested mountains rising on all sides. Such meadows appear to be largely man-made. Grass has replaced cleared forest; tree stumps are scattered over parts of them. They are probably mainly extensions of a few original, naturally open spots, perhaps unforested because of poor drainage. These spots were enlarged during the claim period in cutting forest for mine timbers or to extend the grazing area. Pasture vegetation is dominantly bluegrass, Poa spp., wheat grass, Agropyron spp., and sedges.

The area of desert shrub is most extensive in the
central part of the San Luis valley. The dominant plants
are greasewood, Sarcobatus vermiculatus, rabbit brush,
Chrysothamnus spp., and, much less abundant, the shadscale,
Atriplex canescens. These plants, particularly greasewood,
are generally adapted to highly alkaline soils.
Around the area of greasewood on the floor of the valley
lies a zone of shrubs, mainly rabbit brush and, in the
east and southeast parts of the valley, sage brush,
Artemisia tridentata. Blue grama grass grows on the
slopes just below the foothills in an almost continuous
belt around the valley, meeting and extending into the
pinon-juniper zone at its upper edge. (Hamaley, pp.
239,266.)

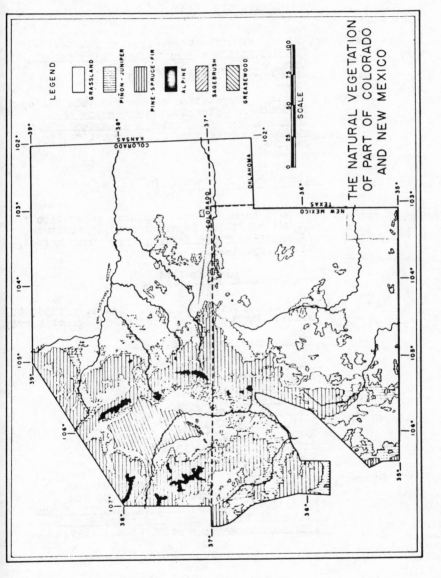

THE NATURAL VEGETATION
OF PART OF COLORADO
AND NEW MEXICO

LEGEND

GRASSLAND
PIÑON - JUNIPER
PINE-SPRUCE-FIR
ALPINE
SAGEBRUSH
GREASEWOOD

SCALE
0 25 50 75 100

51

Literature Cited

Gastetter, Edward F. "The Vegetation of New Mexico," _The University of New Mexico Third Annual Research Lecture._ 13 April 1956. Albuquerque: 1956. p. 268

Rameley, Francis. "Vegetation of the San Luis Valley in Southern Colorado," _University of Colorado Studies. Series D (Physical and Biological Sciences._ III March 1942, pp. 239,266.

Literature Consulted

Shantz. J. L. and Raphael Zon. "Natural Vegetation," in United States Department of Agriculture, _Atlas of American Agriculture._ Washington: 1924. pp. 1-29.

Maps Consulted

Army Map Service. Editions of 1958. Scale: 1:250,000. Printed by the United States Geological Survey

    Albuquerque Sheet. NI 13-1.
    Aztec Sheet, NJ 13-10.
    Dalhart Sheet. NJ 13-12.
    Durango Sheet, NJ 13-7.
    La Junta Sheet. NJ 13-9.
    Lamar Sheet, NJ 13-6.
    Pueblo Sheet, NJ 13-5.
    Raton Sheet, NJ 13-11.
    Santa Fe Sheet. NI 13-2.
    Trinidad Sheet, NJ 13-8
    Tucumcari Sheet. NI 13-3.

Bannett, Henry. "Map of the Cordilleran Region, Showing the Distribution of Woods and Forests," _Nineteenth Annual Report of the United States Geological Survey. Part V (Forest Reserves)._ Washington: 1899.

Hayden, Ferdinand V. Economic Map of Colorado,"
          Tenth Annual Report of the United States Geo-
          logical and Geographical Survey of the Territories
          embracing Colorado and Parts of Adjacent
          Territories, being a Report of Progress of
          the Exploration of the Year 1876. Washington:
          1878. Number Two. Scale: four inches
          equal forty-eight miles.

Marschner, Francis J. "Major Land Use Areas, Western
          United States In United States Department of
          Agriculture, Irrigation Agriculture in the
          West. Miscellaneous Publications 670.
          Washington: 1948. Figure 17 (facing page
          30). Scale: one and thirteen-sixteenth
          inches equal 200 miles.

CHAPTER 5

JICARILLA APACHE USE OF THE LAND

The Jicarilla Apache of mid-19th century made their living mainly from hunting and gathering. Agriculture was locally important.

The buffalo was the chief game animal up until the time of railroads in the claim area. Although buffalo had ranged into the western Rocky Mountains at an earlier date, by this time they were only found eastward, in the plains area. But even on the plains, herds had been almost completely destroyed by commercial hunters. The antelope was the most widely distributed of the large game animals; by 1887, it was probably the most abundant, particularly so in the open plains and valleys. Muledeer and white tailed deer were important game animals then, as now. Elk and the Rocky Mountain Bighorn sheep were hunted in mountainous country; the elk in alpine meadow areas and neighboring forests; the sheep, above the timber line along crests of the Sangre de Cristo.

A great variety of vegetable products were used. The piñon tree is one of the most widely distributed trees in the area, and the piñon nuts were among the most important wild food. Chokeberries, wild plums, yucca fruits, and wild grapes were important too. (Opler, pp. 206.)

Agriculture was more common to the Jicarilla Apache than
is commonly supposed. Maize, beans, and pumpkins were the
principal plants cultivated. Agriculture was most intensively
practiced along the upper Arkansas River, especially along
the Purgatoire and neighboring tributaries. One of the
earliest references to the Jicarilla Apache is that made
in 1706 by the Spanish explorer Juan de Ulibarri. He
encounted Jicarillas to the north of Raton Mesa who informed
him that they were "busy with the sowing of corn, frijoles,
and pumpkins". (Thomas, p. 64.) Later in the neighborhood
of El Cuartelejo, an Apache center, Ulibarri remarks upon
his meeting with Apaches, "They came without arms very happy
and kindly disposed. They brought us much buffalo meat,
roasting ears of Indian corn, tamales, plums and other
things to eat." (Thomas, p. 68.)

The Jicarilla Apaches were perhaps the first plains-
tribe to use horses; they acquired them shortly after the
arrival of the Spanish. Possession of the horse made for
a considerable change in livelyhood. For instance, the
Indians no longer needed to await annual migrations of the
buffalo, but followed the herds northward in summer and
southward in winter. As the various groups encroached upon
each other's territories, inter-tribal warfare became, perhaps
more common. Conflicts over boundaries between the Jicarilla
Apache and other plains groups, the Comanche for example,
are of long standing. These, however, were plainly not
wars of extermination. The bitterest tribal wars and the

56

major changes in tribal territories began later toward the middle of the 19th centure, with the establishment of trading posts, particularly those of Bent on the Arkansas River. The Jicarilla and other tribes began to use new types of clothing, and equipment in exchange for furs and buffalo robes. Economic developments following penetration of the area by American miners, cattlemen and homesteaders culminated in the establishment of U. S. Army forts, decimation of the plains-tribes, and their confinement on reservations. The following rather pathetic historical note, as told by living members of the Jicarilla Apache tribe, shows the plains-Indians at the close of the century completely overwhelmed by events, and not yet fully aware of their actual condition.

57

THE COMANCHE MAKE PEACE

By 1897 railroads and bacbwire criss-crossed the area that had been contested by the Jicarilla and the Comanche. Farmhouses and towns had sprung up by the hundreds, and both tribes had been placed on reservations. The Comanche then decided to make peace with the Jicarilla Apache enemy. A party of about twenty-five Comanche men and women, mounted on buck skin mules, set out from Herman, Oklahoma for Dulce, New Mexico.

The Apache heard of their coming and prepared a war party. Aspen poles were cut for sham lances. Saddles, clothes, and other white man's gear were set aside. Warriors smeared their faces and chests with white paint, made from a sulfurous rock common in the Jemez Mountains and with black mud from the lake bottom. The rounded up their best horses, dappled the white ones with black paint, and made themselves fierce in every way possible. In the meantime the women prepared a feast.

The war party came upon the Comanche near
Horse Lake. Approaching at a gallop they rode
round and round shouting insults and pretending
to stab with the aspen lances. The Comanche
women, overcome with a sense of realism, began
screaming and weeping. Then, submitted to a
whipping, as Apache victory-custom dictates; some
old Apache women, remembering parents killed and
children stolen, whipped too hard and had to be
restrained. Two or three who came with knives were
disarmed and dragged away. After this, the Comanche
were given a prolonged feast and many presents,
including fresh horses. Apache children
and poor people who could offer nothing else,
gave a stick as a token present.

The Comanche had stayed about a week when
a U. S. Government agent came up to Dulce and
ordered them home, reminding them that they had
come without permission.

58

Literature Cited

Castetter, E. F. and Bell, W. H. *The Aboriginal Utilization of the Tall Cacti in the American Southwest.* Ethnobiological Studies in the American Southwest, IV Biol. Ser., Vol. 5 no. 5.

Forbes, Jack D. "The Appearance of the Mounted Indian in the Northern Mexico and the Southwest to 1680" *Southwestern Journal of Anthropology.* Vol. 15, pp. 189-212, 1959.

Opler, M. E. *A Summary of Jicarilla Apache Culture.* American Anthropologist, Vol. 38, pp. 202-223, 1936.

Thomas, Alfred B. *After Coronado, Spanish Exploration Northeast of New Mexico. 1696-1727,* ,1935.

Literature Consulted

Hyde, George E. *Indians of the High Plains, From the Prehistoric Period to the Coming of Europeans.* 1959.

Newcomb, W. H. Jr. "A Re-examination of the Causes of Plains Warfare" *American Anthropologist,* Vol. 52, pp. 317 330, 1950.

Standley, Paul C. *Some Useful Native Plants of New Mexico.* Annual Report of the Smithsonian Institution for 1911. pp. 447-463.

CHAPTER 6

EARLY SETTLEMENT AND COMMERCE

Before the nineteenth century, American knowledge
of the geography of the claim area was slight. During
the first half of the century, information became available
from a number of sources. There were official reports
from military expeditions, for example, those of Zebulon
M. Pike in 1806-07 and Stephen H. Long in 1819-20.
Several accounts by Mountain Men[1] were published. To
these were added the reports of Santa Fe Trail traders,
fur traders, and private explorers. The main physical
features of the area were known by 1840.

61

After news of the California gold discovery reached
the east coast in 1849, traffic through the claim area
increased greatly. As production of the California mines
diminished, news of discoveries of gold and silver came
from New Mexico, Colorado, and elsewhere in the Rockies.

The activities of traders, miners and cattlemen gave
rise to widespread changes in Indian tribal boundaries .

---

[1]The term was first used by Francis Parkman, The Oregon
Trail, and George Ruxton, Adventures. By Mountain Men,
Parkman meant fur trappers west of the Missouri River,
especially in the Rocky Mountains; they commonly met at
the Payou Salade, that is, South Park, Colorado.

and economy. But the event which led to the complete
disruption of Indian occupancy was the opening up of a
vast area of farming land to legal settlement, following
the Homestead Act of 1862. Within a short time the claim
area had experienced remarkable change in occupants and
land use.

MEXICAN SETTLEMENT (1807-1840). When Lieutenant
Pike visited the Spanish colony of Nuevo Mexico in 1807,
Mexican settlements were in the Rio Grande watershed, with
few exceptions. At this time the Mexicans had settled
as far north as Ojo Caliente (Pike, p. 242).

During the first half of the nineteenth century,
Mexican settlement outside the Rio Grande watershed proceeded
very slowly. Probably the first such settlement was Mora,
begun about 1818. The next settlements were San Antonio
and Santa Gertrudis, both founded about 1835. (Chavez,
p. 322.) The founding of Las Vegas, in 1835, probably was
stimulated by development of the Santa Fe Trail.

An observer in the claim area in 1841 reported no
Mexican settlements north of Mora. He remarked that the
principal northern settlements in the Rio Grande Valley
was Arroyo Hondo. (Sage, p. 224.) In 1846, another

observer reported that Rio Colorado was the northern
extension of settlement along the Rio Grande.(Ruxton,
p. 191.) In the southern part of the claim area there were
no towns east of Anton Chico. As late as 1862, Anton
Chico was spoken of as the first settlement met upon
leaving Camp Arbuckle, Oklahoma, for New Mexico. (Marcy,
p. 183.)

Thus, in the mid-19th century, before the principal
period of American immigration, the mortheastern perimeter
of Mexican settlement was weakly established at Anton
Chico, Las Vegas, Mora, and Rio Colorado:

> The valley of the Rio Grande between 37 degrees and
> 32 degrees north latitude, comprises more than
> nine-tenths of all settlements of New Mexico, and
> contains a population of about 50,000 persons. The
> only other settlements in the territory, with the
> exception of three or four small villages west of the
> river, lie along and very near to the great road from
> Santa Fe to Independence, and in no case are found
> farther from the valley of the Rio Grande than
> seventy miles. (Pope, p. 10.)

63

SETTLEMENT 1840-1862. Except for Indians, the
claim area was very sparsely settled before 1840. Most
of the settlers were Mexican, with a few American or
European trappers and traders. Settlement was mainly
along the eastern foothills of the Sangre de Cristo
Mountains.

64

ARMY EXPLORATIONS IN THE CLAIM AREA
1806 TO 1854

PIKE (1806-07)
LONG & BELL (1819-20)
FREMONT (1843-44)
EMORY (1846)
ABERT (1846-47)
MARCY (1849)
BEALE-HEAP (1853)
GUNNISON-BECKWITH (1853)
WHIPPLE (1854)

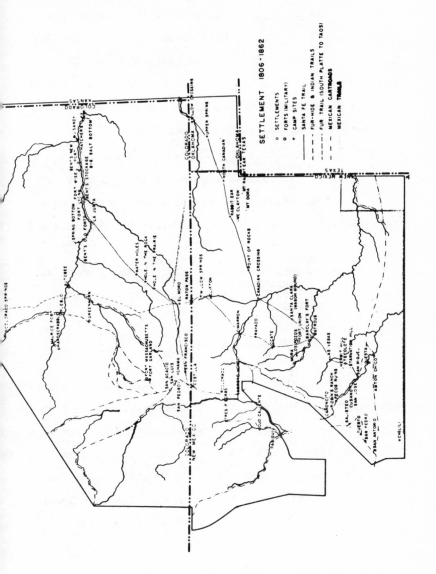

SETTLEMENT 1806-1862

○ SETTLEMENTS
▫ FORTS (MILITARY)
✦ CAMP SITES
— SANTA FE TRAIL
—·— FUR-HIDE & INDIAN TRAILS
—·— FUR TRAIL (SOUTH PLATTE TO TAOS)
····· MEXICAN CARTROADS
≈≈≈ MEXICAN TRAILS

65

The passage of emigrant trains through the claim area on the way to California, beginning in 1849, led to a change in the economic activities of the few settlers there. Men who had been fur trappers, traders, and the like, began to farm areas close to wagon roads so they could barter with the travellers.

Between 1851-1855, a few small Mexican shepherd hamlets came into being along the Culebra River in the lower San Luis Valley. These sites were settled as the sheep industry expanded northward into the San Luis Valley:

> Costilla was a new settlement in 1853; at that time settlers had a few fields of corn, wheat and oats. (Beckwith, p. 39-40.)
> San Luis (La Culebra) was settled in 1851.
> San Pedro, 1852
> San Acacio, 1853
> Chama (Colorado), 1854-55
> San Francisco, 1854-55

66

Fort Union (1851-1891) was established to protect wagon trains going over the Santa Fe Trail. This fort was the major depot for military operations in the Southwest and stimulated local production of hay and food. In contrast to some such outposts elsewhere in the United States, and particularly with regard to the presidios of the Spanish, no permanent settlement grew up around this fort.

THE SANTA FE TRAIL. The Santa Fe Trail was
not on the principal route between the eastern United
States and the far west. Cross-country routes to the
north of the claim area were of greater economic
significance. The Santa Fe Trail was, however, an
important commercial link between the United States and
Mexico, and a major factor in the economic development
of the claim area.

Both Mexican and Americans had attempted to
trade between Missouri, Santa Fe, and Chihuahua before
1807; but it was not until Pike's report that efforts to
establish such a trade became common.

A few Missouri traders succeeded in reaching
Santa Fe before 1821, but most were imprisoned by the
Mexicans; their goods were confiscated.

In 1821, Becknell reached Santa Fe after a
two and one half month journey via the Arkansas and Raton
Pass. Upon his return he reported that merchandise
was arriving in Santa Fe from Vera Cruz; and that the
Mexican traders were making handsome profits.

In 1822, Cooper with a company of fifteen
men transported four to five thousand dollars worth
of goods by pack-horses to Santa Fe. In the same
year, Becknell with thirty men transported five thousand
dollars worth of goods. Becknell and his company were

the first to try the Cimarron cutoff; they were unsuccessful.
Backtracking, they succeeded in reaching the Arkansas
and continued over the older, better-known route.

Before 1825, the main trail had run up the north
side of the Arkansas to Bents Old Fort (Fort William.
Here it crossed the river and continued south to the
Purgatoire, crossing below Trinidad; thence, it ran through
the Baton Pass, then crossed the Canadian, and passed
through the sites of Cimarron, Rayado, Ocate, and Fort
Union. From Fort Union, the trail continued south to
Las Vegas, Tecolote, San Miguel, San Jose, Pecos Ruins
and Santa Fe.

This Bents Fort or Mountain Branch of the Santa
Fe Trail was almost adandoned soon after the Cimarron
Cut-off was established in 1825. In 1854, the Mountain
trail was in such bad condition that Percival G. Lowe
wrote,

> trees had fallen across the trail, mountain torrents
> had made great gulleys, and it took Lieutenant
> Braig's pioneer part--....--several days to make
> the road passable. (Lowe, p. 177.)

During the Civil War, the old Mountain Trail
was again used regularly. The Cimarron Cut-off
was occasionally raided by Confederate guerrillas and
Apaches at this time. (Lowe, p. 387.)

68

The Cimarron Cut-off was never settled. It
was a fast, dry trip on the cutoff from Cimarron, Kansas,
to Las Vegas, New Mexico. Camp sites were at springs
or river crossings.

The first camp sites reached in moving westward
into the claim area along the Cut-off were Willow
Crossing on the Dry Cimarron, and Upper Spring. The
next was on the North Canadian, also known as the McNess
or Corrumpa River.

From the North Canadian, the trail ran past
Rabbit Ear Mounds, and passed close to Mount Dora and Mount
Clayton. Camp sites were on Rabbit Ear Creek and at the
base of Point of Rocks.

Canadian Crossing, a major stop for wagon
trains, was a little south of Taylor Springs. Here
the trail divided; one branch continued south to
Wagon Mound; the other led to Fort Union.

69

Wagon Mound was near the Santa Clara Springs.
The settlement of Santa Clara, later named Wagon Mound,
was founded in 1850. From Wagon Mound, it was an easy
trip to Las Vegas.

As the number of trains using the trail increased,
forage became scarce; the trains began branching out
forming short cut traces. Wagons usually carried

scythes (Lowe, p. 369.), and where grass was abundant,
it was cut and carried for future use; for example, along
the Arkansas for the trip to the Purgatoire River. As
the wagons did not follow the old ruts, the trail in places
was as much as a half a mile wide and never less than
a hundren feet, except in rougher terrain, as near Raton
Pass, where the trail narrowed to the width of a wagon.

Between 1821 and 1846, traffic on the Santa
Fe Trail increased steadily. When Mexican ports were
closed, as in August 1846, trade between Missouri and
Santa Fe was stimulated. That month thirty-nine
companies (413 wagons and 800 men) left Missouri
with nearly a million dollars worth of goods. (Storrs,
Niles Register LXXI, p. 62.)

70

This was the beginning of the period of maximum
traffic on the Santa Fe Trail. The eastern terminal point
which had been at Franklin in the early days was moved
upstream to Fort Osage, Blue Mills, Ducker's Ferry and
to Independence in 1832. West Port, still further west
won most of the ʳoutfitting trade after 1840. Westport
held the position until the railroad arrived. Other towns,
Lawrence, Topeka, and Leavenworth, were minor terminals.

SUMMARY OF TRAFFIC ON THE SANTA FE TRAIL

(PERIOD OF MAXIMUM TRAFFIC)

1850 Westport alone sent out 500 wagons.
1851 549 wagons came into Santa Fe, ranging in trains of seven to forty. (Riddle, p. 12.)
1855 The total Santa Fe trade was estimated at 5,000,000 dollars. (Duffus, p. 244.)
1858 2,440 men, 1,827 wagons, 429 horses, 15,714 oxen, 5,316 mules, 67 carriages and 9,608 tons of goods passed over the trail. The total capital invested was 2,627,300 dollars plus 3,500,000 dollars and traders were arriving daily with gold, silver, furs, pelts, and wool. (Riddle, p. 13)
1859 Trade had risen to 10,000,000 dollars. Between March 1 and July 31, 2,300 men, 1,970 wagons, 840 horses, 4,000 mules, 15,000 oxen, 73 carriages and 1,900 tons of freight had left Missouri. (Riddle, p. 13.)
1860 A total of 9,084 men, 3,033 wagons, 6,147 mules, 27,920 oxen and 16,439,000 pounds of goods left. (Duffus, p. 244.)
1862 3,000 wagons, 618 horses, 20,812 oxen, 6,406 mules, 96 carriages, 3,720 men and 10,000 tons of freight valued at 40,000,000 dollars left Missouri. (Riddle, p. 14.)
1863 The Kansas Pacific (later the Union Pacific) began to lay tracks at Wyandotte, near Kansas City. (Duffus, p. 257.) Nevertheless, for a few more years, the Santa Fe trade continued vigorously.
1865 Between the 12th of May and July 1st, 188 wagons, 2,692 men, 736 horses, 2,904 mules, 15,855 oxen, 56 carriages and 10,489,200 pounds of freight had taken the trail. (Riddle, p. 14.)
1866 No train consisting of less than twenty wagons and thirty armed men was allowed to pass Fort Riley or Larned. Between five and six thousand wagons left for Santa Fe and returned empty or with copper, minerals, or wool. (Riddle, p. 14.)
1868 The eastern terminal for Santa Fe trade moved to Hays City, Kansas.
1876 The Santa Fe trade had its terminal at La Junta and was only hauling 2,000,000 dollars in goods. Three years later the Santa Fe Railroad was in Las Vegas. (Duffus, p. 264.)
1880 The railroad was extended into Santa Fe and the use of the Santa Fe Trail ended. (Duffus, p. 267.)

71

SETTLEMENTS, CAMPSITES, AND LANDMARKS ON THE MOUNTAIN
BRANCH OF THE SANTA FE TRAIL AND THE CIMARRON CUT-OFF.

Big Salt Bottom was usually the first camping
site used by the wagon trains moving westward along
the Arkansas, upon entering what is now Colorado.

Big Sandy Creek Campsite located at the
confluence of the Big Sandy (Sand Creek) and
Arkansas furnished more forage for larger trains.
This was the eastern end of the Big Timbers where
there were "more than the usual amount of cottonwood." The Big Timbers extended about thirteen
miles up the Arkansas and trees were scattered
over the river bottom. (Beckwith, p. 25.)

Hatcher's Trading Post near Willow Creek,
had been abandoned by 1853.

Bent's New Fort and Log Houses, built in 1852
within the Big Timbers, twenty miles down river from
present day Fort Lyon, was abandoned in 1857.
Later Bent leased the Fort and Log Houses to the
government; it was known as Fort Lyon until 1866,
when the fort was moved upstream to the present
site.

72

Bent's Old Fort (Fort William) was built around
1832. Rhia was the last settlement the travellers
saw until they reached Las Vegas. The trip south,
from the Arkansas to the Purgatoire, was difficult.
Water and forage were hard to find.

Water Holes, fifteen miles from the Timpas,
Hole in the Rock, and Hole in the Prairie, were
campsites and water holes.

Raton Pass. Campsites were usually just
north of the pass at El Moro or just to the south
at Willow Springs. In 1866, "Uncle Dick" Wootton,
one of Bent's trappers and traders, built a toll
road across Raton Pass and established his toll
house north of the Colorado-New Mexico line.
The toll house lasted until Santa Fe Railroad
came (1879). (Wootton kept no records.)

Willow Springs, later known as Raton, was
founded as a United States military forage station
in 1860.

Clifton House was built in 1867.

Cimarron began in 1841 as a settlement near the grant of Carlos Beaubien, French trapper and Guadalup Miranda, resident of Santa Fe.

Rayado became a United States military forage station in 1850. Kit Carson settled here in 1849. (Bennétt, p. 16.)

Los Pozos (Holes in the Ground) was the first site of Fort Union built in 1851.

Barclay's Fort was on land acquired in 1849 by Alexander Barclay on which he built a "Fort" and raised crops for sale to trail travellers.

Las Vegas, founded in 1835, was an important post on the trail.

Tecolote was settled in 1824 by Salvador Montoya. Later it beeame a United States military forage station.

San Miguel, was a Mexican settlement.

Pecos Ruins. Before 1838, this had been a regular stop for merchants. A short time later it was abandoned.

Pidgin's (Pigeon's) Ranch, Glorieta Pass, was a United States military forage depot.

Canoncito, later known as Johnson Ranch, was the last stop before reaching Santa Fe.

Literature Cited

Beckwith, Lieutenant E. G. "Report of Exploration of a route for the Pacific Railroad, near the 38th and 39th Parallels of Latitude, from the Mouth of the Kansas to Sevier River, in the Great Basin," in the House of Representatives, Executive Document Number 129. First Session of the Thirty-third Congress. Washington: 1854. XVIII, pp. 1-149.

Bennett, James A. Forts and Forays. James A. Bennett: A Dragoon in New Mexico, 1850-1856. Edited by Clinton E. Brooks and Frank D. Reeve. Albuquerque, 1948.

Chavez, Fray Angelico. "Early Settlement in the Mora Valley," El Palacio, November, 1955.

Daffus, R. L. The Santa Fe Trail. New York, 1930.

we, Percival G. Five Years a Dragoon ('49 to '54) and other Adventures on the Great Plains. Kansas City, 1906.

ke, Zebulon Montgomery. Exploratory Travels through the Western Territories of North America: Comprising a Voyage from St. Louis, on the Mississippi, to the Source of that River, and a Journey through the Interior of Louisianna, and the North-Eastern Provinces of New Spain. Performed in the year 1805, 1806, and 1807. By Order of the Government of the United States. Denver, 1889.

Pope, John. "Report of Exploration of a Route for the Pacific Railroad, near the Thirty-second Parallel of Latitude, from The Red River to the Rio Grande," in The House of Representatives, Executive Document Number 129. First Session of the Thirty-third Congress. Washington, 1854. XVIII, pp. 1-324.

Riddle, Kenyon . Records and Maps of the Old Santa Fe Trail. Raton, 1949.

Ruxton, George F. Adventures in Mexico and the Rocky Mountains. New York, 1848.

Sage, Rufus B. Rocky Mountain Life: or, Startling Scenes and Perilous Adventures. Dayton, no date.

Storrs, Augustus. "Trade Between Missouri and Mexico." Niles' Register, January 15, 1825, XXVII, pp. 312-316.

The Niles' Register. In seventy-five volumes. (The complete set can be found in Bancroft Library, University of California, Berkley.)

Marcy, Randolph B. The Prairie Traveler, A Hand-book for Overland Expeditions. Edited by Richard F. Burton. London, 1863.

Literature Consulted

Emory, William Hemsley. Lieutenant Emory Reports: A Reprint of Lieutenant W. H. Emory's Notes of a Military Reconnoissance. Albuquerque, 1951.

Gregg, Josiah. Scenes and Incidents in the Western Prairies: During Eight Expeditions, and Including a Residence of nearly Nine Years in Northern Mexico. Philadelphia, 1857.

76

CHAPTER 7

TRAPPING, HUNTING, AND TRADING

Little information is available on the amount
of fur collected in the claim area during the years
before Anglo-American occupation. Anglo-Americans found
in Mexican territory were likely to be fined or imprisoned;
often their goods were confiscated. Furs were shipped
from Santa Fe, but traders did not advertise this part of
their cargo.

Nevertheless, until 1824, Anglo-American trappers
and traders outfitted at Taos or Santa Fe, were in the
Sangre de Cristo mountains and along the Rio Grande and
its tributaries. By this time trapping had been almost
given up in these parts. Most of the trappers had moved
westward. In 1846, beaver were still numerous on the
Arkansas and Platte Rivers.[1] But, the best trapping
grounds in the Rockies were to the north of the claim
area, in Bayou Salado and Old and New Parks. (Ruxton,
p. 234.)

---

[1] Beaver skins weigh on the average of two pounds each.
Skins were dried and put in one-hundred pound packs and
carried out by pack animals. In 1837, beaver skins
were selling at seven dollars a pound. (Conard, pp. 54,58f)

Stallo Vinton, editor of Chittenden's
The American Fur Trade, states that after 1831, fur trade
in the Southwest amounted to very little.[2] (Chittenden,
II, p. 974.)

The best known traders in the area were William
and Charles Bent; at one time their trading activities
covered a veritable empire - the larger part of the claim
area. Like most late comers, the Bent brothers found
trapping unprofitable. Nor did they have much part in
the beaver fur trade.

In addition to trading, they engaged in
freighting on the Santa Fe Trail; there they met
Ceran St. Vrain, a Santa Fe merchant. This was the
beginning of the remarkable successful Bent - St. Vrain
partnership.

78

About 1831, the Bents built a permanent post
on the Arkansas. Mexicans, as well as Americans, had
been trading with the Indians, but such trading was
sporadic and unorganized. Bant's post established a
claim of sorts to the land and crowded out lesser
traders.

---

[2] Richard Wootton states that by the fall of 1840
"trapping had....become less profitable...prices of
peltry of all kinds had gone down, and from that time
on I paid less attention to it." (Conrad, p. 85.)
Ruxton states that decrease in the price of beaver was
caused by availability of substitutes such as fur-seal,
sea otter, hare, rabbit and silk. Beaver by 1846 had
dropped from six to eight dollars a pound to one dollar.
(Ruxton, p. 231.)

A second post was built farther down the
Arkansas, in the vicinity of Big Timbers in 1849. This
post was more successful than the first because of its
more central location. Routes from the plains to the
north and south, from the Rockies, from Taos and Santa
Fe converged toward this spot. It was in an ideal location
for trading with the Indians and with commercial buffalo
hunters; many of the latter wintered at Big Timbers.
From this post the Bents could carry heavy shipments of
skins and robes to Missouri without crossing mountains.

Buffalo abounded. Pike had seen them all along
the Arkansas:

> I will not attempt to describe the droves of animals
> we now saw on our route. Suffice it to say that
> the face of the prairie was covered with them on each
> side of the river (Arkansas). Their number exceeded
> imagination. (Pike, p. 68. Pike wrote this
> in November 1805, approximately eighty-three miles
> east of the Colorado-Kansas boundary.)

79

Long's expedition in 1820 reported them north
and south of the Arkansas, in the mountain passes of
Colorado, and in the northeastern part of New Mexico.
(James, III, p. 83.)

Whipple saw signs of buffalo along the Canadian
just east of the New Mexico-Texas border in 1854.
(Whipple, p. 34.)

The Bents, principal shippers of hides and
robes, employed about sixty men. Fifteen to twenty
took buffalo robes and specie to Missouri. The rest were
sent to trade with the Indians, to obtain buffalo meat
for the fort, and to guard animals. (Farnham, p. 163.)
Trade with the Indians was on a barter basis.[1]

After moving down river in 1849 to Bent's
New Fort (later Old Fort Lyon) at Big Timbers, the
Bents began freighting for the Government over the
Santa Fe Trail and catering to emigrant trains going
to the California gold fields. Indian trade was
diminishing. They adandoned this post in 1857 and built
another on the Purgatoire in 1859. It lasted until
Charles Bent's death in 1869.

By 1866, the buffalo were confined between the
western-most Anglo-American settlements and the Rocky
Mountains; they were seldom seen south of the Red River.

---

[1] Morgan gave the following list of prices.

Tariff of American Fur Company, 1833-59

1 Buffalo Robe	=Standard of Value
1 Cup Sugar	=1 Robe
1 Lb. Tobacco	=1 "
1 cup coffee	=1 "
1 gun	=10 "
2½ Lb. Blanket	=3 "
1 saddle	=6 "
1 bridle	=1 "
2 knives	=1 "
25 loads ammunition	=1 "
¾ yard scarlet cloth	=1 "
1½ Calico	=1 "
3 Lb. Blanket	=4 "
1 gallon kettle	=1 "
2 " "	=2 "
3 " "	=3 "
10 " "	=10 "

He remarks that after 1859, prices were higher; one
robe brought three cups of sugar and one cup of coffee.
(Morgan, p. 179.) Dodge adds that by 1872 a robe
was worth from seven to nine cups of sugar. (Dodge,
p. 362.)

In these years, some 40,000 to 100,000 robes were
marketed annually; it was estimated that one buffalo
robe was sent to market for every five skins. (Marcy,
pp. 338f; Dodge, p. 143.) Although a good part of such
trade items originated in the claim area, it is probably
impossible to determine the actual percentage. The arrival
of the railroads greatly increased the export of hides.
Dodge estimates that over a quarter of a million buffalo
hides were carried by the Atchison, Topeka and Santa Fe
Railroad in the single year 1873.

Mexican traders (Comancheros) and hunters.

Trading and hunting were not restricted to Americans.
From an early date, Mexicans had been trading and hunting
in the San Luis Valley, along the Arkansas and Platte,
and had participated much in the Santa Fe trade. Like
the Pueblo Indians, they were trading with Indians
in the plains area to the east.

> Some twelve or fifteen Mexicans were at this time
> present at the Fort (Lancaster, just east of the
> present town of Longmont, Colorado). They constituted
> a trading party from Taos, escorting a caravan of
> pack horses and mules, laden with flour, corn,
> bread, beans, onions, dried pumpkin, salt, and pepper,
> to barter for robes, skins, furs, meat, moccasins,
> bows and arrows, ammunition, guns, coffee, calico,
> cloth, tobacco, and old clothes, which were to
> compose their return freight." (Sage, p. 211.)

In September 1854, Whipple met a number of
Mexican and Pueblo trading parties going into Texas or
to the eastern border of New Mexico to trade flour and
tobacco with the Plains Indians for buffalo robes and
horses. (Whipple, pp. 31f.)

Literature Cited and Consulted

Beckwith, Lieutenant E. G. "Report of Exploration of
a route for the Pacific Railroad, near the 38th and
39th Parallels of Latitude, from the mouth of the
Kansas to Sevier River, in the Great Basin." in
The House of Representatives, Executive Document
Number 129, First Session of the Thirty-third
Congress. Washington, 1854. XVIII, pp. 1-149.

Chittenden, Hiram Martin. The American Fur Trade of
the Far West. New York, 1935.

Conard, Howard Louis. "Uncle Dick" Wootton, The Pioneer
Frontiersman of the Rocky Mountain Region. An account
of the Adventures and Thrilling Experiences of the
Most Noted American Hunter, Trapper, Guide, Scout,
and Indian Fighter now living. Chicago, 1890.

Dodge, Richard Irving. The Hunting Grounds of the Great
West. A Description of the Plains, Game and Indians
of the Great North American Desert. London, 1877.

Farnham, Thomas J. "Travels in the Great Western Prairies,
The Anahuac and Rocky Mountains, and in the Oregon
Territory," Early Western Travels, 1748-1846.
Edited by Reuben Gold Thwaites. Cleveland, 1906.
Vol. XXVIII.

Heap, Givinn. "Central Route to the Pacific," The Far
West and the Rockies Historical Series, 1820-1875.
Edited by LeRoy R. Hafen and Ann W. Hafen. Glendale,
1957. Volume VII.

James, Edwin. "Expedition from Pittsburgh to the Rocky
Mountains," Early Western Travels, 1748-1846.
Edited by Reuben Gold Thwaites. Cleveland, 1905.
Volume XVI.

Lavender, David, Bent's Fort. New York, 1954.

83

Marcy, Randolph B. Thirty Years of Army Life on the Border, Comprising Descriptions of the Indian Nomads of the Plains; Explorations of New Territory; A Trip across the Rocky Mountains in the Winter; Descriptions of the Habits of Different Animals Found in the West, and the Methods of Hunting Them; with Incidents in the Life of Different Frontier Men, etc., etc. New York, 1866.

Morgan, Lewis Henry. The Indian Journals, 1852-62. Edited by Leslie A. White and Clyde Walton. Ann Arbor, 1959.

Niles' Register. In seventy-five volumes.

Pike, Zebulon Montgomery. The Southwestern Expedition of Zebulon M. Pike. Edited by Milo Milton Quaife. Chicago, 1925.

Ruxton, George B. Adventures in Mexico and the Rocky Mountains, New York, 1848.

Sage, Rufus B. Rocky Mountain Life: or, Startling Scenes and Perilous Adventures. Dayton, no date.

Whipple, A. W. "Route near the thirty-fifth Parallel, Under the Command of Lietu. A. W. Whipple, topographical Engineers, in 1853 and 1854," in United States Senate Executive Document Number 78, Second Session of the Thirty-third Congress, Washington, 1856. Volume III.

84

CHAPTER 8

LAND CLASSIFICATION UNDER THE WHEELER
AND HAYDEN SURVEYS

By the 1870's, the geography of the claim area was well known. Its principal mineral resources had been discovered. Much of the area had been evaluated in terms of agricultural and other landuse potentialities.

The classification of lands under the Wheeler survey was started in 1872. Mapping in the claim area was done between 1872 and 1878. Special personnel, topographers, were included in the survey parties to take measurements, make examinations, and gather the notes required by the land classification system. This duty was condidered an important part of the regular field work.

The maps of the Wheeler survey are part of an official report prepared from detail gathered by experienced field parties.

Six dividions were used in classifying the land:

1. Arable or agricultural land: land arable

without irrigation; irrigable land, i.e.
sufficient water available for irrigation.

2. Timber land: large timber; small timber;
prevailing tree species.

3. Pasturage or grazing land: good or poor;
species and quality of grasses.

4. Arid or barren land: including extreme
desert or saline areas.

5. Swamp land and land subject to tidal overflow.

6. Sites of valuable mineral deposits.

Of these six classifications, only four were
used in printing the atlas sheets; namely (1) Arable
or agricultural land; (2) Timberland; (3) Pasturage or
grazing land; and (4) Arid or barren land.

The atlas sheets are on a scale of one inch
to eight miles; the quarter atlas sheets are on a scale
of one inch to four miles.

A description of the atlas sheets and quarter
atlas sheets dealing with the claim area follows. The
descriptions are found in several of Captain George M.
Wheeler's publications, principally in his Geographical
Report, of 1889.

86

Sheets 70A and 70C

Location - Part of southeast Colorado and northeast New
Mexico

Scale - one inch equals four miles

Mapped - 1874-1876

The extents of sheets 70A and 70C are as follows:
Sheet 70A from 104 degrees 7' 30" to 105 degrees 30' 0"
west longitude, and from 36 degrees 30' to 37 degrees
20' north latitude; Sheet 70C from 104 degrees 7' 30"
to 105 degrees 30' 0" west longitude, and from 35 degrees
40' to 36 degrees 30' north latitude.

The area covered by sheets 70A and 70C is mainly
mountain and plateau; it includes a small part of the
plains. The ranges are in the western part of the area,
with plateaus extending eastward into the plains. The
main drainage basins are those of the Purgatory, Canadian,
and Mora and Pecos Rivers.

Sheet 70A covers 1,367 square miles of mountainous area, 1,093 square miles of plateau, 1,094 square
miles of valley land, and 874 square miles of plains.
Sheet 70C covers 1,040 square miles of mountains, 520
square miles of plateau, 260 square miles of valley land,
and 2,600 square miles of plains.

87

Sheet 77B

Location - Central New Mexico

Scale - one inch to four miles

Mapped - 1872-1878

Sheet 77B extends from 105 degrees 30' 0" to
106 degrees 52' 30" west longitude and from 34 degrees
50' to 35 degrees 40' north latitude.

The area is mainly plateaus and mesas; part
of the Rio Grande Valley is shown, and part of the
Jemez Mountains.

Sheet 77B covers 1,172 square miles of
mountainous area, 1,160 square miles of plateau, 984
square miles of valley land, and 1,150 square miles of
desert or barren land.

Sheet 78A

Location - Northern New Mexico

Scale - one inch to four miles

Mapped - 1874-1875

     Sheet 78A extends from 104 degrees 7' 30"
to 105 degrees 30' 0" west longitude, and from 34 degrees
50' to 35 degrees 40' north latitude.

     The area between the Pecos and the Canadian
River is shown. Plateau and plains dominate the area.
Valleys are mainly narrow and within plateaus and mesas.
Little land is completely barren. There are no mountain
ranges in this area. (Wheeler, pp. 223-224.)

88

     HAYDEN SURVEY. The methods used by Hayden
in gathering the information which appears on his economic
map of Colorado for the year 1876 were similar to those
used by Wheeler. In addition to topographic detail,
field crews made the notes needed for the classification
of the land according to potential use. For some
catagories of the use-classification, the map nearly
represents the actual use at the time of the survey.
The following are the types of surface distinguished on
Hayden's map.

    1. Agricultural land; i. e. tillable land
        where water was thought to be sufficient
        for crops, either rain-water or ibrigation
        water.

2. Pasture land.

3. Pine forest. Arable land within this area is limited to small patches, as is grazing land, though with slightly greater extent.

4. Pinon pines and Cedars; of some use for grazing.

5. Quaking aspen groves; Hayden notes that this is largely regrowth area; the aspen appears quickly on areas that have been cleared by forest fires.

6. Sage and badland.

7. Areas above timber line.

All of the Colorado portion of the claim area is shown on Hayden's map.

The American interest in, and knowledge of, valuable minerals of the claim area are plainly indicated on both Hayden's and Wheeler's maps. Hayden's map notes the location of coal lands, gold districts, and silver districts.

89

TABULAR SUMMARY OF LAND CLASSIFICATION

ON WHEELERS' MAPS OF THE CLAIM AREA

Quarter Atlas Sheet No.	No. of Sq. Mi. Classified	Arable or Agriculture	% of Area	Pasture or Grazing
70A	4,373.7	168.0	3.9	1,412.0
70C[1]	4,420.2	155.0	3.5	2,797.2
77B[1]	4,465.9	193.0	4.3	2,537.9
78A	4,465.9	84.0	1.9	3,430.2

Quarter Atlas Sheet No.	% of Area	Timber	% of Area	Arid or Barren	% of Area
70A	32.3	2,536.7	58.0	257.0	5.9
70C[1]	63.3	1,328.0	30.1	140.0	3.2
77B[1]	56.8	1,015.0	22.7	720.0	16.1
78A	76.8	804.5	18.0	147.1	3.3

[1] Partly within the claim area.

90

(Annual Report for 1879 upon the Geographical Surveys of the Territory of the U.S. west of the 100th meridian by Capt. George M. Wheeler - Appendix OO.)

Literature Cited

Tenth Annual Report of the U.S. Geological and Geographical Survey of the Territories, embracing Colorado and Parts of Adjacent Territories. Report of 1876 by F. V. Hayden. Washington: 1878 (See Part II - topography. Report on The Primary Triangulation of Colorado, and Report on the Arable and Pasture Lands of Colorado.)

Report upon U.S. Geographical Surveys west of the 100th Meridian in charge of Captain George M. Wheeler. Volume I, Geographical Report. Washington, 1889.

91

92

CHAPTER 9

LIVESTOCK INDUSTRY

After the Civil War, there was a marked shortage of livestock in the eastern United States. The western Great Plains became a major supply area. The extension of the railroads westward made the rapid shipment of cattle possible.

In the early days of the western cattle industry, land was occupied with little or no legal justification; it was considered free for the taking. Many ranches began with an immigrant's claiming a water hole, buying up a few half-wild cattle, and extending his range as the herd grew. The herds were driven to rail heads in the northeast for sale. By 1872, however, there were few examples of ranches being obtained in this way.

Between 1872 and 1880, there was a general improvement in range stock, as competition with a revived eastern cattle industry grew. The market for western cattle increased further between 1876 and 1880. Packing plants were built in the margins of the Plains; in St. Louis, Kansas City, and Chicago.

During the early years of the 1880's (1880-1885), the Plains experienced a boom in cattle production.

The winter of 1881-1882 was a mild one; cattle flourished
and fortunes were made. Books appeared depicting the
economic prospects for settlers in the Plains in
extravagant terms.[1] Easterners, and a number of
British, Canadians, and Germans began to move into the
area.

In 1883, a drought occurred. The ranges were
probably overstocked. Nevertheless, the cattle business
prospered until 1885. In 1885, there was unusually little
grass and water. Furthermore, grazing was being restricted
by agriculturalist settlers and their barbed wire enclosures.
By this time the Homestead Act of 1862 had finally begun
to affect the western Plains; barbed wire, invented in
94   1872, became the symbol of homesteading. These new
settlers took legal claim of the land; and a number
of the larger cattle empires were broken up.

Cattlemen suffered still another misfortune:
cattle which had sold for nine dollars and thirty-five
cents per hundred weight in 1882 brought one dollar
per hundred weight in 1887 on the Chicago market.
(Webb, pp. 205,269.)

----

[1] Some of the best examples of these "get-rich books" are:
General James S. Brisbin, The Beef Bonanza; or, How to
Get Rich on the Plains, 1881; and, Walter Baron von
Richthofen, Cattle Raising on the Plains, 1885.

Thus the growth of the livestock industry was
affected by economic conditions, winter weather, and
summer drought. At first there had also been raids
by Indians to contend with (Conard, pp. 223 and 424),
but by the middle 1870's most of the raiding had stopped.
Between 1870 and 1880 there was more than a 390 percent
increase in the number of cattle in Colorado (Census,
880, p. 51), which may be attributed in part to the
essening of Indian raids.

New Mexico had a severe winter in 1885-86,
followed by a hot and dry summer, and poor grazing conditions. Cattle were forced on the market at reduced
prices. Another bad winter (1887-1888) followed.
Thus the 1890 census records only a slight gain in the
number of cattle over 1880. The number of sheep in
Colfax, Mora, and San Miguel Counties (258,012) was
less than one half what it had been in 1880.

Periodically blizzards and droughts caused
considerable fluctuation in the number of livestock.
In 1877-1878 the heavy snows
were estimated to have caused over a twenty percent
loss in sheep. The next year a drought occurred which
lasted until July 1880; more than 150,000 cattle had
to be driven out of Colorado. The following winter
in Colorado was the worst in human recollection. (Census,
1880, p. 49.) Between 1888 and 1890, Colorado had a
severe drought which greatly damaged the livestock industry.
(Stewart, p. 123.)

95

Sheep played a minor role in the early ranching economy over most of the Plains; but they were of great importance in New Mexico.

Sheepraising has a long history in Spanish colonies, where environmental conditions permitted its practice. Thus, sheepraising was a traditional feature of the New Mexican economy. The best known Spanish breed, the merino, was jealously guarded against export from Spain. An older Spanish breed - the Churro - was sent to the colonies. The Churro was small and tough, bred to withstand climatic extremes. It became the foundation stock of the New Mexican flocks.[2]

Several types had developed in the Southwest; they were called "native" cattle. The more common types in New Mexico were the Wild Cattle, Texas, Mexican or Spanish and Chino or Curly-haired Texan.[3]

During Spanish and Mexican occupation, sheep were for long periods the most significant export of New

---

[2]The Churro was later referred to as the New Mexican by Anglo-Americans; at present, it is known as the Navajo
[3]Wild Cattle were brown with a lighter stripe running down their backs; they had long, slim, blue horns. The Texan was usually multicolored with patches of white. The horns were thin and enormously long with a half twist back. Heads were thin and coarse. The body, tall and gaunt with narrow hind quarters. Legs were long and hoofs large.
Mexican or Spanish Cattle were smaller than the Texas. They were raw boned with shorter horns. They were often black and white but sometimes in brindle, brown, or calico.
Chino or Curley-haired Texan were large, heavy, well-formed animals with medium-sized horns. They were usuall brownish buffalo in color; in winter the hair became curly. (Tenth Census, 1880 p. 36.)

Mexico. Between 1820 and 1830, as many as 200,000

head were driven annually to Mexico. In the 1840's,

it appears that the number of sheep and goats, had

been reduced by Indian raids. In 1843, Josiah Gregg wrote:

> But the <u>Ganado Menor</u>, or small beasts of pasture,
> (that is, sheep and goats in general), have of late
> been very much reduced in quantity; having suffered
> to a deplorable extent from the frequent "inroads
> of the aboriginal 'lords of the soil'.", who every
> now and then, whenever hunger or caprice prompts
> them, attack the ranches, murder the shepherds;
> and drive the sheep away in flocks of thousands.
> Indeed, the Indians have been heard to observe, that
> they would long before have destroyed every sheep
> in the country, but that they prefer leaving a few
> behind for breeding purposes, in order that their
> Mexican shepherds may raise them new supplies!
> (Gregg, p. 190.)

The same conditions were said to prevail in

1852 (Exec. Doc. No 65; p. 350.), and until as late as

1879:

> The ranching business of that section (Canadian,
> Pecos rivers and their tributaries) of the country
> was greatly retarded until the last six years by
> the proximity of the plains Indians. Then, when
> the danger no longer existed it rapidly filled
> up with herds.... (Mills, p. 25.)

Sheep were introduced into Colorado

in 1850 by the New Mexicans. They were grown along the

stream courses, near the boundary between New Mexico

and Colorado. Until 1865, sheep raising was predominantly

in the hands of Mexicans. (Census, 1880, p. 52.)

Sheep ranges were in the more arid parts of southeastern Colorado, and along the east and west sides of the San Luis Valley, especially east of the Rio Grande and south of Fort Garland. The average value of these ranges was twelve cents an acre. (Census, 1880, p. 53.)

Between 5 February 1879 and 12 July 1880, New Mexico ranges suffered from a drought. Sheep perished by the thousands; the loss was estimated at twenty-five to fifty percent. Nevertheless, the 1880 census reported over one half million sheep in Colfax, Mora, and San Miguel Counties. Colfax County was stocked tto full capacity in 1880. The census noted that ranges were not as good as they had been ten or even five years previously. Then too, cattle raising was growing in relative importance over sheep raising in the northeastern part of New Mexico.

Seventy-two percent of the sheep in Colax, Mora, and San Miguel counties were still New Mexican (Churro). By this time some merino stock had been introduced and the remaining twenty-eight percent were various mixtures of merino with the older breeds; the merino and mixed breeds were of greater value than the New Mexican.

Flocks in the northeast of New Mexico were not shifted around much but were kept on farms until ready for market. Then most of them were driven to Kansas for sale.

By 1890, Colorado had fewer sheep than in 1880.
Probably the principal causes for the decrease in sheep
population were deterioration in range quality (from over-
stocking), change in sheep breed, and the increased competition
of the sheep industry in the northwestern United States. Cattle,
on the other hand, increased over 1880.

99

Literature Cited

Bancroft, Hubert Howe. "History of Nevada, Colorado, and Wyoming, 1540-1888," The Works of Hubert Howe Bancroft. San Francisco, 1890. Vol. XXV.

Conard, Howard Louis. "Uncle Dick" Wootton, The Pioneer Frontiersman of the Rocky Mountain Region. An Account of the Adventures and Thrilling Experiences of the Most Noted American Hunter, Trapper, Guide, Scout, and Indian Fighter now living. Chicago, 1890.

Gregg, Josiah. Scenes and Incidents in the Western Prairies: During Eight Expeditions, and Including a Residence of nearly nine years in Northern Mexico. Philadelphia, 1857. In two volumes.

Mills, T. B. San Miguel County, New Mexico, Illustrated. Las Vegas, 1885.

Stewart, George. "History of Range Use," in United States Senate, The Western Range, Document Number 199, Second Session of the Seventy-fourth Congress. Washington, 1936.

United States Department of Interior.
Seventh Census, 1850 (Statistics of Territories).
Eighth Census, 1860 (Agriculture of the United States in 1860).
Ninth Census, 1870 (The Statistics of the Wealth and Industry of the United States).
Tenth Census, 1880 (Report on the Productions of Agriculture.
Eleventh Census, 1890 (Report on the Statistics of Agriculture in the United States).

Webb, Walter Prescott. The Great Plains. New York: 1931.

CHAPTER 10

AGRICULTURE

Agriculture in the New Mexico portion
of the claim area may be discussed under three regional
subdivisions: agriculture of the intermontane
valleys and high plateaus; agriculture of the eastern
plains area; and, the agriculture of the irrigated
river valleys.

1. The intermontane valley and high plateau
farming areas are largely within the present-day counties
of Colfax, Mora, San Miguel, Santa Fe, Taos,
and Rio Arriba. Here both irrigation and dry farming
were practiced. The principal crops were beans, corn,
wheat, oras, barley, and hay; potatoes being grown
at the highor elevations.

The more important valleys are the following:
the Moreno Valley in Colfax County (dry farming of
potatoes, cereals and vegetables); The Mora River
Valley in Mora County (the growing of cereals, hay,
vegetables, and apples under irrigation); The
Taos Valley in Taos County known as the "Granary of
New Mexico". Wheat, field peas, and hay were grown
here under irrigation .

2. Dry farming was practiced to some extent, mainly during the 1880's, before the drought of 1893 to 1895. (Hunter, Colorado, p. 8; New Mexico, p. 11.) The dry .arming was concentrated in the area of present-day Union, Harding, and Quay counties. The major crops were corn, wheat, and sorghums.

3. The important irrigated river valley areas were the Pecos, Canadian, and Gallinas River valleys (in San Miguel county). Among the principal crops were wheat, oats, barley, beans, corn, hay, garden vegetables, and fruit.

IRRIGATION. Irrigation was practiced by the Indians of New Mexico before the arrival of Europeans. Early Spanish settlers irrigated land along the Rio Grande in New Mexico. The custom spread northward and eastward in New Mexico with the spread of settlement. Yet irrigation was practiced principally in the neighborhood of the Rio Grande; elsewhere there were localized areas of irrigation agriculture along the lower courses of streams heading in the Sangre de Cristo -- for example, in the Mora Valley (Eleventh Census, 1890, pp. 193-201).

Following is a resume of irrigation agriculture as it had developed in the claim area by 1890.

102

Colfax County - Irrigation was highly developed.
here were two canals with lateral systems, and a
umber of reservoirs for storage of flood waters.

The Springer system headed on Cimarron Creek. The
ain canal of this system was ten miles long by twenty
eet wide at the bottom; it had forty miles of lateral
itches. This system aupplied water to land between the
imarron and Red Rivers.

The Vermejo system obtained water from Vermejo Creek.
he main canal was twelve miles long by twenty feet wide;
t had about forty-five miles of lateral ditches. The
and supplied with water was to the west of Dorsey and
axwell. Reservoirs stored runoff water from summer
loods. Both of these systems were started by the
axwell Land Grant Company. The surveys were made in 1887.
onstruction began in 1888; the two systems were completed
n 1893. (Coan, p. 469.)

103

Mora County - In 1890, this county contained the
argest amount of irrigated land in New Mexico (approxi-
ately one-half of one percent of the county). The main
rea of irrigation was in the Mora River Valley. However,
he supply of water was adequate only in the upper part
f the valley. Ocate Creek also supplied irrigation
ater for a considerable area.

San Miguel County - Here the water was supplied
mainly by the Pecos and Sapello Rivers and their tributaries.
The Sapello did not furnish sufficient water for the land
then under cultivation; the water supplied by the Pecos
water was adequate except in its lower reaches in the
county.

Taos County - The greater part of the land under
irrigation received water from Taos and Embudo Creeks.
The land was much subdivided; small irrigable sites were
located along the creek bottoms.

Las Animas County

The principal streams in the county are the Apishapa
River, Timpas Creek, and the Purgatoire River. Irrigation
104 was commonly practiced near the headwaters of the rivers
in the spring. There the land only requires irrigating
once to give a fair yield of hay. The larger irrigation
ditches receive their water from the Purgatoire River.

1. Duran and Vigil ditch

Source - 6 miles south of Stonewall from the
south side of the south fork of the
Pugatoire.

Length - 4 miles long by 3 feet wide

Cost - $1500

640 acres were under irrigation in 1889.

2. Chititi ditch

Source - 1 mile east of Trinidad on the south
side of the Purgatoire.

Length - 3 miles and 4 feet wide

Cost - $2000

Started - 1861 (finished in 1861)

Already by 1890, the Mexican system of sub-division of family lands among heirs had much reduced the size of individual holdings. The fields were strips, commonly some 25 to 300 yards wide and up to 1000 yards long, usually at right angles to the river course. The outer ends of the strips usually had access to an irrigation ditch.

105

Literature Cited

Coan, Charles F. <u>History of New Mexico</u>, 3 Vols. 1925

Siebenthal, C. E. <u>Geology and Water Resources of the San Luis Valley, Colorado</u>. USGS Water Supply Paper #240. 1910.

Steinel, Alvin T. <u>History of Agriculture in Colorado, 1858 to 1926.</u> The State Agricultural College, Fort Collins, August 1, 1926.

<u>Irrigation Agriculture in the West</u>. U. S. Department of Agriculture Miscellaneous Publication #670. U. S. Government Printing Office: 1948.

Literature Consulted

Newell, F. H. <u>Report on Agriculture by Irrigation in the Western Part of the United States</u>. Department of the Interior; Census Office. The 11th Census of the United States, Vol. 5. 1890.

Holmes, J. Garnett. <u>Soil Survey of the San Luis Valley, Colorado</u>. U. S. Department of Agriculture, Bureau of Soils. Field operations of the Bureau of Soils. 1903 (5th report). Washington: Government Printing Office. 1904.

U. S. Census Reports -- 1850-1890.

Hunter, Byron. <u>Type of Farming and Ranching Areas in New Mexico, Part 1</u>. Bulletin 261, Agricultural Experiment Station of the New Mexico College of Agriculture and Mechanic Arts, May, 1939.

Linney, C. E., F. Garcia, and E. C. Hollinger. <u>Climate as it Affects Crops and Ranges in New Mexico.</u> Bulletin 182, Agricultural Experiment Station of the New Mexico College of Agriculture and Mechanic Arts, March, 1930.

106

CHAPTER 11

THE RAILROADS

The Santa Fe railroad entered the claim area in
1878. By providing transportation for importing
mining equipment and exporting minerals, the railroad
attracted investors and helped create the great mining
development of the 1870's. By linking the plains with
markets in the east, it helped bring on the cattle
boom of the 1880's. By advertising and recruiting,
the railroad encouaged the influx of homesteaders and
other settlers, thus stimulating agricultural development in the area. Rail service gave the area a new
value.

The only railroad to enter the revised claim area
was the Atchison, Topeka, and Santa Fe. It came to
link the cities and resources of the Arkansas Valley
with those of the upper Canadian and Pecos valleys,
as well as those of the Rio Grande Valley, and connected
these with markets on the west and east coasts.

A comparison of rail and stage fares, as given in
the table below, indicates that the per mile passenger
fares were often only half as much on the railroads
as on the stage lines. Until it was displaced entirely,

stage travel augmented rather than competed with rail transportation.

By the time rails reached the claim area, Granger pressure on Congress had forced discontinuance of land grants to railroads, and the last land was so granted in 1871. (Hibbard, 1924, pp. 249,250). No federal land grants were awarded for rail construction within the claim area.

The railroads did, however, receive rights-of-way and small tracts adjacent thereto, for shops and stations, as well as the use of certain resources for construction purposes.

A law of March 3, 1875, affecting the Atchison, Topeka, and Santa Fe, the Denver and Rio Grande, and some smaller corporations, provided that roads should be granted right-of-way,

> to the extent of one hundred feet on each side
> of the central line of said road; also the
> right to take from the public lands adjacent
> to the line of said road material, earth, stone,
> and timber necessary for the construction of
> said railroad; also grounds adjacent to such
> right-or-was for station buildings, depots,
> machine shops, side-tracks, turn-outs, and water
> stations, not to exceed in amount twenty acres
> for each station, to the extent of one station
> for each ten miles of road. (18 Stat., p.482,
> March 3, 1875, quoted in Donaldson, 1884, p.
> 941.)

Given this access to public resources, the railroads used local timbers in virtually all their construction work. (Campbell, 1922, p. 29.) Local mineral fuels were used also. (Table ⅙.)

The entry of the railroad raised land prices considerably. Lands fronting on railroads commanded a better price than others; a speculative fever spread with each rumor of prospective railroad construction.

In New Mexico, an official of the General Land Office reported in 1880 that "the advent of the Atchison, Topeka, and Santa Fe Railroad has advanced rents 100 per cent." (Annual Report of the Commissioner of the General Land office, 1881, p. 29.) The same report noted the general optimism engendered by the railroad's arrival:

> the completion of the New Mexico and Southern Pacific Railroad to Santa Fe...and the completion of the grading of the Denver and Rio Grande Railroad, whose track has been laid to within 45 miles of Santa Fe, have infused new life into all departments of trade, and the business outlook is flattering. (Annjal Report of the Commissioner of the General Land Office, 1880, p. 30.)

With the increasing growth of settlements along the railways, there emerged a need for urban transportation; during the 1880's "street railway" companies, using animal power, incorporated in two of the claim area's towns: Trinidad and Las Vegas.

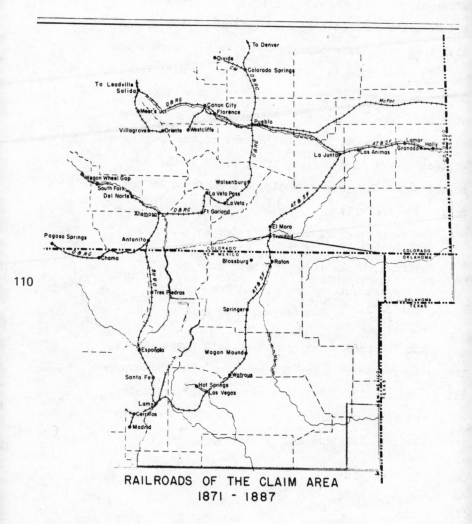

RAILROADS OF THE CLAIM AREA
1871 - 1887

RAILROAD CONSTRUCTION IN THE CLAIM AREA

Date	Major Line	Orig.Co.	Route Constructed	Mileage
1878	AT&SF	P&AV	Las Animas to N.M. state line via La Junta	112
	AT&SF	NM&SP	New Mexico state line to Raton	14
1879	AT&SF	NM&SP	Raton to Las Vegas	112
	AT&SF	NM&SP	Las Vegas to Lamy	64
1880	AT&SF	NM&SP	Lamy to Santa Fe	18
	AT&SF	NM&SP	Lamy to Cerrillos.	18
1882	AT&SF	NM	Raton to Blossburg	5
	AT&SF	NM	Las Vegas to Hot Springs	6
	AT&SF	NM	Cerrillos to Madrid	3

Sources: Campbell, 1922; Coan, 1928, pp. 247-252; Darton, 1915; Henderson, 1926, p. 61; Poor's 1888, pp. 734, 753-55, 796; and Ritch, 1885, pp. 13-18. Abbreviations: AT&SF, Atchison, Topeka, and Santa Fe; P&AV, Pueblo and Arkansas Valley: NM&SP, New Mexico and Southern Pacific; NM, New Mexican

===

REPRESENTATIVE RAILWAY FARE
ca. 1880

	Fare	Mileage	Average Fare
Kansas City to Santa Fe	$41.00	870	.04 per mile

111

REPRESENTATIVE : STAGE : FARE
ca. 1880

	Fare	Mileage	Average Fare
Alamosa to Santa Fe	$28.00	141	.19 per mile

Source: Frank Fossett, COLORADO, TOURIST'S GUIDE TO THE ROCKY MOUNTAINS, New York, 1880, p. 72,26.

SOME EXPENDITURES BY ROADS FOR THE ATCHISON,
TOPEKA, AND SANTA FE[1] (during year 1887)

For Real Estate and Permanent Improvements on Auxiliary Roads:

Pueblo and Arkansas Valley RR........$29,703[2]
New Mexico and So. Pacific RR........ 36,254[2]
New Mexican RR...................... 34,852[2]

For Real Estate and Construction of New Roads:

Pueblo and Arkansas Valley RR
(Clelland Extension: Clelland
to Canon City, incl. 2 coal
spurs, 10.3 miles)...................$211,836[2]

Other Expenditures:

Canon City Coal Co....................$92,000
Las Vegas Hot Springs Hotel
and Bath Houses........................ 78,746

112

---

[1] Poor's Manual of Railroads, 1888, H. V. and H. W. Poor, New York, 1888, pp. 739-740.

[2] Road extends outside claim area; breakdown of expenditures not given.

FUEL CONSUMED BY LOCOMOTIVES OF THE ATCHISON, TOPEKA, AND SANTA FE[1]
during the year ending June 30, 1880)

Kind		Source	Quantity	Average Cost
Coal	bituminous	Kansas, Colorado	120,000 tons	$1.85 ton
Wood	pine, cedar, etc.	Kansas, Colorado New Mexico	2500 cords	2.50 cord

[1] Tenth Census of the United States, 1880, Part IV, Transportation, Government Printing Office, Washington.1883, p. 580.

STREET RAILWAYS[a]

(figures for the year July 1, 1889- July 1, 1890)

	Trinidad Street Railway	Las Vegas St. R'way
Date of Corporate Charter[b]	Feb. 22, 1886	Dec.20, 1880
Mileage [b]	2.5	1.5
Total Passengers Carried	75,000	90,000
Motive Power[b]	Animal	Animal
Horses and Mules[c]		
Total Number	26	11
Total Cost	$3000	$1300
Employees[d]	7	7
Cost of Land & Buildings[e]	$18,300	$5,500
Taxes & Licenses [f]	$80	$135

[a] Eleventh Census of the United States, 1890, Part I. - Transportation, Government Printing Office, Washington, 1895.
[b] Ibid., pp. 705,709.
[c] Ibid., pp. 782,785.
[d] Ibid., pp. 756,762.
[e] Ibid., pp. 714, 717, 731, 737.
[f] Ibid., pp. 815,821.

Literature Consulted

Annual Report of the Commissioner of the General Land
    Office, 1880. Government Printing Office, Washington
    1881.

Bradley, Glenn D. The Story of the Santa Fe, The Gorham
    Press, Boston, 1920.

Campbell, Marius R. Guidebook of the Western United
    States. Part C.. The Santa Fe Route, USGS Bull.,
    613, Government Printing Office, Washington, 1915.

Coan, Charles F. A Shorter History of New Mexico, Part
    II, Edwards Brothers, Ann Arbor, 1928.

Darton, N. H. Guidebook of the Western United States,
    Part C.. The Santa Fe Route, USGS BULL. 613,
    Government Printing Office, Washington, 1915.

Donaldson, Thomas. The Public Domain, Government Printing
    Office, Washington, 1884.

Eleventh Census of the United States, 1890, Part I.
    Transportation, Government Printing Office, Washingto
    1895.

Fossett, Frank. Colorado, Tourist's Guide to the Rocky
    Mountains. New York, 1880.

Hall, Frank. History of the State of Colorado, Vol. 2,
    Blakely Printing Co., Chicago, 1890.

Henderson, Charles W. Mining in Colorado, USGS
    Professional Paper 138, Government Printing Office,
    Washington, 1920.

Hibbard, Benjamin Horace. A History of the Public Land
    Policies. MacMillan, New York, 1924.

Poor's Manual of Railroads, 1888. H. V. and H. W. Poor,
    New York, 1888.

Ritch, William G. The History, Resourced and Attractions
    of New Mexico. D. Lothrop and Co. Boston, 1885.

Tenth Census of the United States, 1880. Vol. IV,
    Transportation, Government Printing Office, Washington,
    1883.

114

Davis, E. O. The First Five Years of the Railroad Era in
    Colorado, Sage Books, Inc., 1948.

Dunbar, Seymour. A History of Travel in America, Vol. IV, Bobbs-
    Merrill, Indianapolis, 1915.

Greever, William S. Arid Domain: The Santa Fe Railway and Its
    Western Land Grant, Stanford University Press, Stanford, 1954.

Matthews, William B. Matthews' Guide, Lowdermilk & Co., Washington,
    1889.

Mosk, Sanford A. Land Tenure Problems in the Santa Fe Railroad
    Grant Area, University of California Press, 1944.

Sanborn, John Bell. "Congressional Grants of Land in Aid of Rail-
    ways," Bulletin of the University of Wisconsin, No. 30, August,
    1899.

Van Arsdale, Jonathan. "Railroads in New Mexico," Research,
    University of New Mexico, December, 1937.

Waters, L. L. Steel Rails to Santa Fe, University of Kansas Press,
    Lawrence, 1950.

CHAPTER 12

MINING AND INDUSTRY

The principal mineral products for the period 1843-1887 were
gold and silver, with copper, lead, iron, and coal coming into
production toward the close of the period as railroads arrived and
industry developed. Zinco ores were known to be plentiful but were
little mined because no economical process of extraction was known.

The Spaniards were the first Europeans to enter the area in
search of precious metals. The Indians probably had mined little
but turquoise. The Pueblo Indain revolt of 1680 interrupted Spanish
mining in the area until the nineteenth century.

Moreno-Ute District

The boundary of the revised claim area runs through the Moreno
Valley from Eagle Nest Lake to Black Lake. Thus some of the mining
locations described below are within the area and some are without.

Gold, the major product of this district, was discovered at
Willow Creek in 1866 (Jones, p. 161; Lindgren, p. 92). This area
was at one time within the Spanish land grant of Beaubien and
Miranda. It later became property of the Maxwell Land Grant Company.

The district produced some two and a quarter million dollars in

placer gold, and a lode production of about the same amount
up to January 1904. (Lindgren, et.al., p. 93, and pp.
96,97; Jones, p. 145;) Ore worth one million dollars was
extracted from a single mine, the Aztec mine, during its
first four years of operation, 1868-1872. (Jones, p. 150.)

As a large amount of water was needed, the Moreno Water
and Mining Company began construction of a ditch to carry water
from the Red River to Grouse Gulch and Humbug Gulch. The
digging of the ditch was begun in May, 1868, and practically
completed by November of the same year. The ditch was a
little over forty-one miles long and cost $210,000. An
additional $20,000 was spent in constructing reservoirs
at the headwaters of the Red River. (Jones, p. 145; and
118 Raymond, 1869-70, p. 392.) The first water delivered was to
Humbug Gulch on July 9, 1869, and sold for fifty cents a
miner's inch (one and a half cubic feet per minute). By
1870, six additional, though smaller, ditches were operating
in the district. (Raymond, 1869-70, pp. 392ff.)

The more important areas of placer and lode mining in
the district during the period 1848-1887 were Willow Gulch,
Mexican Gulch, Grouse Gulch, Humbug Gulch, Spanish Bar,
Moreno Valley, and Ute Creek. A description of mining in
these areas follows:

Willow Gulch

Claims owned by Arthur and Company in Willow Gulch were

mined in 1867. The opening of the claims, construction of ditches and a reservoir, and building construction cost about $14,000. During the first season, between April and November of 1868, the company recovered 400 ounces of gold, worth $8000 (currency). The amount recovered between April and August of the following year was 464 ounces, worth $10,347. (Raymond, 1869-70, pp. 389f.)

Upslope from the Arthur and Company claims on Willow Creek were the claims of Middleton and Company, Union Company, Idaho Company and Dutch Johns'. Below Arthur and Company claims were the Eureka Company, Harrison and Company, and O. K. Company. The latter two claims were not opened.

Mexican Gulch

The neighboring Mexican Gulch was rich in gold, but had no water ditch in 1870. (Raymond, 1869-70, p. 391.)

119

Grouse Gulch

Carpenter's property had eight claims, each 300 feet square. The cost of opening the claim was $8,000. From May 10, 1869 to October 18, 1869, they washed 1700 cubic feet of gravel and recovered over 142 ounces of gold ($22.20 per ounce).

Calhoun's claim was 1250 feet long. 6200 dollars in gold was recovered in 1868, 200 dollars during six weeks of work in the spring of 1869.

Other claims in Grouse Gulch were the following: Malloy and Company, Riley and Company, Bergman, Ned Pointer, Michigan Company, Pollack claim. (Raymond, 1869-70, pp. 393f)

Humbug Gulch

In Humbug Gulch were: Martin and Scott claim, Faulkner
and Coleman claim, California claim, and Bergman's claim.
Raymond, 1869-70, pp. 394f.)

Spanish Bar

Spanish Bar is situated just below the mouth of Grouse
Gulch and on the opposite side of the Moreno River. The
gold was sluiced from the river banks at a height of
from twenty to thirty feet above the river bed.

Moreno Valley

Very little mining was done within the Moreno Valley
proper, between 1848 and 1887. According to Lindgren,
dredging was carried on here in the early 1900's.
(Raymond, 1869-70, p. 395.) In the Moreno district the most
important group of claims was the Red Bandana group with
some 2,000 feet of workings. (F. A. Jones, p. 150.)

Dates of discovery and operation are not given for the
other mining properties in the area.

Ute Creek

The Ute Creek area was worked considerably. The gold
was much coarser here, and probably derived from the
vicinity of the Aztec lode. (Lindgren, p. 105.)

An estimate of the production of the placer deposits in
the district from the time of their discovery in 1866 through
December 1903 is given as $2,250,000. (Jones, p. 145.)

The lode mine production was estimated as being over two
million dollars up to 1910. (Lindgren, p. 93.)

The Aztec mine, the richest and one of the oldest in
the district, was discovered in the spring of 1868. It is
situated between Ute Creek and the Ponil River. The mine
consisted of several tunnels and shafts dug to a maximum
depth of 220 feet and a length of a thousand feet. (Lindgren,
p. 97.) In 1868, a fifteen-stamp mill was erected at a
cost of eight thousand dollars. A 1675 foot tramway for
hauling ore connected the main tunnel with the mill.
(Raymond, 1869-70, p. 386.) Products of this mine were
estimated to have been worth about one million dollars during
the first four years of operation. The total production up
to 1910 was one and a quarter to one and a half million
dollars. (Lindgren, p. 97.) The ore of average quality from
this mine ranged in value from five to seventy dollars per ton.
(Lindgren, p. 97.) Extraction and milling costs in the district
were estimated at from ten to twenty dollars per ton.
(Raymond, 1869-70, pp. 386ff.)

Two other claims, the Montezuma and the Bull of the
Woods, produced a fairly large amount of ore. The Montezuma
claim is situated near Camp Baldy on the east slope of Baldy
Mountain with the Bull of the Woods claim adjoining it. Up
to 1910, the estimated production of the Montezuma claim
was about $300,000. (Lindgren, p. 98.) In 1869, Lucius B.
Maxwell, the principal shareholder in the Montezuma claim,

121

began installing a thirty-stamp mill. By the end of the year, about 600 tons of ore had been mined. Ore yield was seventy-five dollars per ton on the stamp. (Raymond, 1869-70, p. 387)

Numerous other mines operated in the area; one of these was the French Henry mine on the French Henry Mountain. Its development included a fifteen-stamp mill and 2,700 foot aerial tramway. (Lindgren, p. 99.)

The following is a record of mines producing in the Moreno-Ute district on January 1, 1872. (From R. W. Raymond, reported by M. Bloomfield):

Exhibit of producing mines in Moreno mining district, Colfax County, New Mexico, on January 1, 1872, Reported by M. Bloomfield.

Name	Owner	Character	Course	Dip	Dimensions	Country-rock
Willow Creek	6 companies	Placer	Gravel	--	2 mi. x 300 ft.	-------
Moreno Creek	3 companies	--do--	--do--	--	½ mi. x 300 feet	River diggings
Grouse Gulch	7 companies	--do--	--do--	--	2 mi. x 300 feet	--------
Humbug Gulch	5 companies	--do--	--do--	--	1½ mi. x 300 feet	--------
Last Chance	1 company	--do--	--do--	--	2000 ft. x 300 ft.	--------
New Orleans Flat	1 company	--do--	--do--	--	1500 ft. x 300 ft.	--------
Aztec Mine	Aztec Mining Company	Lode	NW & SE	--	3000 feet	Slate
Montezuma	Maxwell Land-grant & Railway Company	--do--	--do--	--	3000 feet	Granite
Chester	Graham, Dimick & Co.	--do--	--do--	--	3000 feet	--do--

		Vein-matter	Ore	Average Value	Mills	Product for year ending 1-1-1872
Willow Creek	6 companies	---	--	Unknown	--	$40,000
Moreno Creek	3 companies	---	--	--do--	--	40,000
Grouse Gulch	7 companies	---	--	--do--	--	80,000
Humbug Gulch	5 companies	---	--	--do--	--	25,000
Last Chance	1 company	---	--	--do--	--	10,000
New Orleans Flat	1 company	---	--	--do--	--	5,000
Aztec Mine	Aztec Mining Company	Quartz	--	--do--	15 stamps	Unknown
Montezuma	Maxwell Land-grant & Railway Company	--do--	--	--do--	30 stamps	Idle .. all year
Chester	Graham, Dimick & Co.	--do--	--	--do--	25 stamps	Unknown

123

Lesser metals and non-metals

There was a small production of other metals at other locations in the Sangre de Cristo mountains, such as in the Pecos Canyon and near Glorieta.

In New Mexico iron ore had probably been found at Iron Mountain in Colfax County and at Glorieta Mesa in San Miguel County during the latter part of the period 1848-1887. The only producer recorded is the Kennedy mine on Glorietta Mesa. Probably several thousand tons of good quality ore have been mined from this locality. The dates of discovery and production are not given for either area. (Lindgren, pp. 102 and 112.)

Another area prospected in the early 1880's was Willow Creek district in San Miguel County. The Pecos mine (then known as the Hamilton mine) was located in 1882. The area was not fully developed until early 1927. The chief ores taken from the mine were those of zinc, lead, copper, gold, and silver. (Anderson, p. 111.)

The Red River district, located around the town of Red River in the Sangre de Cristo Mountains, was prospected in 1869. Gold was discovered in both placer and lode deposits, along with lead and copper. A smelter was built in 1879 at Red River, but it was not successful. Up until 1920, the district had not produced a great amount of ore.

124

As for the non-metallic minerals, mica, gypsum, salt, cement, gem stones, and sulphur were produced in small quantities. Their importance was largely local (Jones, pp. 289-312). Mica, for example, was used for window glass in New Mexico; it was produced in the claim area at the village of Talco, in Mora County (Jones, p. 260).

Coal

Coal was the only mineral fuel produced in the claim area up to 1887. The producing area is still known as the Raton coal district, but within it were two separate fields. The Trinidad field, of Las Animas and Huerfano counties, Colorado, produced 1,157,969 tons in the two years 1886-1887; the coal was worth about one dollar and sixty cents a ton (Min. Res. 1888, p. 229,230; Richardson, p. 436). The other principal coal field in the Raton Mesa district was the Raton field in Colfax County, New Mexico. Production of this field amounted to 684,816 tons for the period 1882 to 1887; the coal was worth about one dollar and thirty cents per ton. (Min. Res. 1892, p. 440.) Both of these fields produced bituminous coal. Some was used for making coke, but probably the larger part was bought for fuel by the railroads.

125

The Raton coal field which covers an extensive part of
Colfax County was mainly developed in the vicinity of Raton
up to 1887. The mines at Dawson, and Koehler were not
developed until later.

The old Gardiner mine (formerly the Blossburg Number 4)
was located in Gardiner Canyon by the Atchison, Topeka and
Santa Fe Railroad about 1882 when the railroad first entered
New Mexico in this area. (USGS Bull., #752, p. 94.) The
Atchison, Topeka and Santa Fe Railroad operated the mine
until 1896. The Blossburg mine was operated by the Raton
Coal and Coke Company (Incorporated August 29, 1881), which
developed the earlier mines. (Coan, p.459.) Another
mine, the old Dutchman located between Seeley and Dutchman
Canyons, was also an early producer. (Bull, #752, p. 94.)
These mines (Gardiner, Bloosburg, and old Dutchman) have
produced as much as 400,000 tons of coal a year, although
this production had not been attained by 1887. (Bull.
#752, p. 110.) Coal had been mined commercially there
since the early seventies, but production records are
not available before 1882. The average value of the coal
in 1892 was about one dollar and thirty cents per ton.
(Mineral Resources of the U.S., Bulletin #752, p. 251.)

The Trinidad coal field located along the eastern base
of the Front Range was the largest producer in the claim
area during the period, 1848-1887.

126

The two oldest mines in the district were the Engle
and the Starkville, both within a few miles of Trinidad.
The mines were owned by the Trinidad Coal and Coking Company.
(Bull. #381, p. 396.) The El Moro mines, six miles south
of El Moro, Colorado, were owned by the Colorado Coal and
Iron Company (now the Colorado Fuel and Iron Company).
These mines were the largest producers in the area for a
number of years. (Min. Res., 1888, p. 230.) The El
Moro mines produced 58,904 tons of bituminous coking
coal in 1880. Part of the coal was sold to the Rio
Grande Railroad, the rest was sold in Denver, Colorado
Springs, Canon City, and other towns in Colorado. (10th
Census, Vol. 15, pp. 867f.)

Two other mines located near Trinidad, the Rifenburg
mine and the mine owned by the Trinidad Coal Mining
Company, produced 20,160 tons of bituminous coking coal
each in 1880; it was shipped to Topeka. (10th Census, Vol.
15, pp. 867f.)

In 1888 production in Las Animas and Fremont counties
increased markedly. For example, production in Las
Animas County increased forty percent over 1887 because
of the opening of new mines. (Min. Res., 1888; pp. 229
and 230; Bull. #381, p. 436.) Between 1886 and 1888, the
production of the Trinidad field amounted to 2,024,034 tons.
Min. Res., 1891, p. 216; USGS Bull., #381, p. 446.)

127

The value of the coal from this field was about
one dollar and sixty cents per ton. (Min. Res., 1892.)
Much of the coal produced in the Trinidad field was
manufactured into coke of excellent quality.

The Raton Mesa coal region has been mainly developed
along its eastern boundary where the coal beds are exposed
in the walls of the Park Plateau canyons and in the
sediments at the edges of lava-capped mesas. The coal varies
from coking bituminous type in the southern part of the
field to semi-coking, and domestic-bituminous types in the
more northerly areas.

The coal production for Colorado and New Mexico, as
128 given in the annual issues of <u>Mineral Resources of the</u>

United States follows:

New Mexico Recorded Coal Production for 1882-1887 (Short Tons)

Year	Raton	Los Cerrillos	Monero
1882	91,798	3600	12,000
1883	112,089	3000	17,000
1884	102,513	3000	11,203
1885	135,833	1000	14,958
1886	87,708	1000	7,000
1887	154,875	7500	11,000
Comparison) 1888	227,427	25,200	12,000
Total: 1882-1887	884,816	19,100	73,161

Colorado Recorded Coal Production for 1873-1887 (Short Tons)

Year	Location	Short Tons [129]
1873	Las Animas & Fremont Counties	12,187
1874	Las Animas & Fremont Counties	18,092
1875	Las Animas & Fremont Counties	15,278
1876	Las Animas & Fremont Counties	20,316
1877		
1878	Central Division[1]	73,137
	Southern Division	39,668
1879	Central Division	70,647
	Southern Division	60,455
1880	Central Division	136,020
	Southern Division	126,403
1881	Central Division	174,882
	Southern Division	269,045
1882	Central Division	160,000
	Southern Division	466,385

Year	Location	Short Ton
1883	Central Division	280,345
	Southern Division	488,618
1884	Central Division	296,188
	Southern Division	483,865
1885	Central Division	327,038
	Southern Division	553,172
1886	Sentral Division	332,024
	Southern Division	519,619
1887	Central Division	417,326
	Southern Division	638,350

---

[1] The Central and Southern Division for 1878 throught 1884 include the following coal mining areas: Central division: Sedalia, Franceville, Como, Canon City (produced more than the other three); Southern division: Trinidad, and El Moro, Walsenburg, Durango, and Rico (produced much less than Walsenburg).

130

COKE PRODUCTION

Colorado was the fifth ranking producer in the nited States from 1884 through 1887. The yearly production nd value per ton for the whole state from 1880 to 1887 s as follows:

Year	Short Tons	Value(per ton)
1880	25,568	$5.68
1881	48,587	5.29
1882	102,105	4.67

Three areas of coke production are represented in ese figures. They are the Trinidad district, the largest roducer, and the Crested Butte and Durango districts ich are not situated in the claim area. For 1887, the rinidad district produced some 127,602 tons of coke from 36 coke ovens. In 1880, Colorado had only 200 coke ovens; y 1887, the number had increased to 532.

The average yield of coke from the coal used creased from forty-nine percent in 1880 to sixty-four rcent in 1887 for the state as a whole. (Min. Res. 382-1887.)

132

MINING DISTRICTS

A. ORTIZ MINE GRANT
   1. Cerrillos (Ag, Pb, Zn)
   2. Old Placers (Au)
   3. New Placers (Au)

B. MONERO-UTE CREEK
   4. Elizabethtown-Monero (Au)
   5. Ute Creek (Au)

C. PLATERO-SUMMITVILLE
   6. Platero (Ag)
   7. Summitville (Au)

D. ROSITA-SILVER CLIFF
   8. Rosita (Ag)
   9. Silver Cliff (Ag)

E. SMALLER DISTRICTS
   10. Grape Creek (Fe)
   11. Hot Springs (Fe)
   12. Grayback-Russell (Fe, Au)
   13. Kerber Creek (Au)
   14. Red River (Au)
   15. Pecos-Willow Creek (Pb, Zn)
   16. Nacimiento (Cu)
   17. Glorieta (Fe)

F. COAL MINING DISTRICTS
   a. Cerrillos District
   b. Monero District
   c. Canon City District
   d. Walsenburg District
   e. Trinidad District
   f. Raton District

Literature Cited

Anderson, Eugene C. *The Metal Resources of New Mexico and Their Economic Features through 1954.* State Bureau of Mines and Mineral Resources. New Mexico Institute of Mining and Technology. Bull. #39. 1957.

Emmons, S. F. *The Mines of Custer County, Colorado.* Seventeenth Annual Report of the United States Geological Survey, Part II, 1896.

Fossett, Frank, *Colorado (Tourist's Guide to the Rocky Mountains).* New York, 1880.

Henderson, Charles W. *Mining in Colorado.* Dept. of the Interior, United States Geological Survey, Professional Paper 138. Washington, D. C. 1926.

Jones, Fayette A. *New Mexico Mines and Minerals.* Worlds Fair Edition, 1904.

_____. *Coal Resources of the Raton Coal Field, Colfax County, New Mexico.* United States Geological Survey Bull. #752, 1924.

Lindgren, Waldemar, Louis C. Graton, and Charles H. Gordon. *The Ore Deposits of New Mexico.* Dept. of the Interior, United States Geological Survey, Professional Paper #68. 1910.

Mineral Resources of the United States. Dept. of the Interior, United States Geological Survey. 1882-1892.

Patton, Horace, B., and others. *Geology of the Grayback Mining District, Costilla County, Colorado.* Colorado State Geological Survey, Bull. #2. 1910.

Patton, Horace B. Geology and Ore Deposits of the Bonanza District, Saguache County, Colorado State Geological Survey, Bull. #9. 1915.

_____. Geology and Ore Deposits of the Platoro-Summitville Mining District, Colorado. Colorado State Geological Survey, Bull. #13. 1917.

133

Pumpelly, Raphael. Report on the Mining Industries of the
United States, with special investigations into the
iron resources of the Republic and into the cretaceous
coals of the Northwest. Dept. of the Interior,
Census Office. The 10th Census of the United States,
Volume 15. 1880.

Raymond, Rossiter W. Statistics of Mines and Mining in
the United States and Territories West of the Rocky
Mountains. Printed in the following House Executive
Documents:
Serial #   Printed:
1424. 41st Cong., 2nd Session. Ex. Doc. 207-1869-70
1513. 42nd Cong., 2nd Session. Ex. Doc. 211-1871-72
1601. 43rd Cong., 1st Session. Ex. Doc. 141-1873-74
1608. 43rd Cong., 2nd Session. Ex. Doc. 177-1874-75

Richardson, G. B. The Trinidad Coal Field, Colorado.
United States Geological Survey, Bull. #381, Part II,
Mineral fuels. 1910.

Schrader, F. C. The Durango-Gallup Coal Field of
Colorado and New Mexico. United States Geological
Survey, Bull. #285. 1906.

The Oil and Gas Fields of Colorado. Rocky Mountain
Association of Geologists, 1954.

134

CHAPTER 13

TIMBER AND FOREST PRODUCTS

The woodlands of the foot-hills and mesas supplied fuel and fence material for local use at an early date. But with the arrival of the railroad the lumber industry expanded greatly, or at least the industry's potential increased. Fir and pine were used for mine timbers and for railroad ties, and they were obtained mainly from the lower more accessible mountain slopes.

Furthermore, large quantities of wood from New Mexico and Colorado were made into charcoal in local kilns and used as fuel by the railroads before the development of coke manufacturing (10th Census, Vol. IV, p. 580).

In 1880 the amount of lumber sawed in New Mexico was small; it came mainly from San Miguel and Santa Fe counties. Most of the better-grade lumber came by rail from Chicago. However, the potentialities of the area for lumber production were clearly recognized; in the U. S. Census report of 1880:

> The coniferous forests of these mountains are dense and valuable, and although not yet accessible for lumbering operations except at a few points, they seem destined to become an important factor in the future development of the whole region. They can, if properly protected, supply with lumber indefinitely a larger population than will probably occupy this part of the United States. (10th Census, Vol. IX, p. 563)

Sawmills were in operation well before the 1880 census. The maps drawn by the Wheeler survey of New Mexico and Colorado for 1874-1876 show sawmill locations (for example at Santa Mina on Manuelitos Creek, just south of the Mora Valley, shown on Atlas Sheet 70c). The locations of three sawmills are noted on a map of Colfax County by Lewis Kingman, C. E., drawn in 1876. The mills were near the head of the Red River, near the head of the Cimarroncito River, and near the junction of Moreno Creek and Cenigilla Creek.

Regarding the cost of lumber and mining timber, about the year 1870 in the Moreno mining district, wood cost $2.35 per cord at the mill; lumber and mining timbers cost $30.00 and $15.00 per thousand feet respectively. (R. W. Raymond, 1869-70, pp. 366 and 388.)

In New Mexico, "during the census year (1880), 64,034 acres of woodland only were reported destroyed by fire, with an estimated loss of $142,075." (10th Census, vol. IX, p. 568.) Here the value placed upon the woodland vegetation (probably mainly ponderosa pine, pinon, and juniper) in New Mexico, in the U. S. Census report, is somewhat over two dollars per acre.

Certainly the growth of the lumber industry was closely associated with the expansion of the railroad--in the railroad's use of timber and lumber and fuel, and in the accessiblility and possibility that rail transport gave for developing the industry.

Literature Cited

Raymond, Rossiter W. <u>Statistics of Mines and Mining in the States and Territories West of the Rocky Mountains</u>. Printed in the following House Executive Document: Serial #1424. 41st Congress, Second Session. Ex. Doc. 207 - 1869 to 1870 (Printed 1870).

<u>Tenth Census of the United States, 1880</u>.
Vol. IV, Transportation. United States Government Printing Office. Washington, 1883.
Vol. IX, Forests of North America. United States Government Printing Office, Washington, 1884.

138

SETTLEMENT UNDER THE LANDACTS. Several U.S.
Government landacts, particularly the Five Year Homestead
Act and The Timber Culture Act, stimulated settlement
of the claim area after 1862. In Colorado, the areas
most affected were in Baca, Prowers, Pueblo and Bent
Counties (reference is made here to present county
boundaries). In New Mexico, less settlement occurred;
the areas of the present counties, Union, Colfax, Harding,
Santa Fe, and Quay were the major centers. By far the
larger part of settlement under the landacts took place
between 1880 and 1887, particularly toward the end of
that period.

RECORDS AVAILABLE

NEW MEXICO (for the claim area only). Homestead
entries for the claim area of New Mexico are on file in the
Public Room, Bureau of Land Management, Federal Court House
Building, Santa Fe, New Mexico. On May 1, 1959, the
Bureau replaced the original tract records with a new set
of record books. The new tract books were used in this
study. They are much easier to read than the old books
and give the same descriptive information, (except that the
names of the claimants are deleted). The books give
the following information for each entry: section;
location with section, description of outlying lots which
may be involved with the claim entry; type of entry,
number of acres, date of final letter or patent (serial
or order number), and statement of cancellation or
relinquishment. The new records are in chronological
order; tracts are filed by range, and arranged by
quadrants.

COLORADO (for the claim area only). Records for
Colorado are filed in the Public Room, Bureau of Land
Management, New Customs House, Denver Colorado. These
tract records are the original filings. Persons searching

140

them for the purposes of this study found the work slow
and tedious. Some of the entries are illegible; several
could not be tabulated bacause of poor conditions of
the tract books.

They contain the same information as the books for
New Mexico, and in addition, the names of the claimants.
In some cases loans, mortgages and appraisals upon the
claims are noted.

Claims are listed by range, township and section,
and filed under the names of old district land offices,
e.g., Hugo, Lamar, Pueblo.

141

TOWNSHIP AND RANGE

Historical Background

The rectangular system of public surveys was
adopted in 1785 during the administration of Thomas
Jefferson. It grew out of the old town grants of the
Massachusetts Colony, which first organized the system
in 1634 to allot land grants (six miles square) suitable
for plantations.

The new system was designed to protect public lands,
to provide a better method of land description, to clarify
land titles, to establish a system of land-title records,
and to promote orderly settlement, forcing settlers to
take poor as well as good land.

By 1899, twenty-four Initial Points, intersections
of Principal Meridian Lines with Base Lines (or surveying
meridians) were in use. The New Mexico Meridian and Initial
Point was established in 1848. The Sixth Principal Meridian,
which controls surveying in Colorado, was established in
1861.

From the Initial Point, townships six miles square
run and are numbered, north and south of the Base Line
(see figure 1) along the Principal Meridian. Numbered
ranges also begin at the Initial Point and run east and
west of the Principal Meridian along the Base Line.

Township boundaries are oriented due north and south,
east and west. Boundaries running north and south are
termed range lines and boundaries running east and west
are township lines. Thus, the subtitles of township and
range are location lines. An area cannot be located
either by township or range alone, but must include both.

Townships are divided into thirty-six sections, i.e.
thirty-six square miles. (see figure 2)

County

Tracts are listed by township and range, not by counties in New Mexico. In recording the data for this study, the names of present day counties were added for each entry. This was also done for Colorado.

For Colorado the designation tract book was used. When tract records were moved to the regional office in Denver, each set of records kept the name of its particular area land office. For the claim area the following tract records were found under: Pueblo, Book 1 to 27; Lamar, Book 1 to 15; and Hugo, Book 1 to 14. No page numbers were given; listings are by range, township and section.

143

LOCATION

Section (principal subdivisions of a township)

Each township is divided into thirty-six sections, each one mile square or approximately 640 acres, and laid out in checker-board fashion. Beginning at the northeast corner, each section is numbered one through thirty-six (as shown in figure 2).

Quartering. The sections may be divided into quarters: northwest[2], southwest[2], northeast[2], and southeast[2]. Each quarter-section contains approximately 160 acres (see figure 3).

<u>Quarter-quarters</u>. Quarter-sections may be further sub-
divided into quarters: northwest^4, southwest^4, northeast^4,
and southeast^4, (see figure 3), each containing about forty
acres.

    <u>Lots</u>. In some cases lots were claimed. These are
irregular parcels of land, the smallest subdivisions
of a section.

    On the New Mexico data sheets, a regular quartering
and sub-quartering system was used, corresponding with
the tract records. No quartering system was used on the
Colorado data sheets because the record on locations was
written out and entry locations wil correspond to figure
3.

144

GRANTEE

    The word Grantee on the New Mexico data sheets was
not used as a sub-title. The space, instead, was used
for dates of cancellations or relinquishments (left hand
side) and serial numbers of the claim (on the right hand
side).

TYPES OF ENTRIES

    The following is a list of the types of entries
made within the claim area between 1860 and 1887:
Congress by enacting the <u>Cash and Credit Sale Land Law</u>
of May 18, 1796 (1 stat. 464.), and May 10, 1880 (2 stat.
13)

gave settlers the chance to buy land either for cash or on credit. The Act of April 24, 1820 (3 stat. 566) repealed the credit sales and provided for the sale of land (in lots as small as 80 acres) at public auction. Lands unsold at auction were then open for private sale at a minimum price, finally fixed at one dollar and twenty-five cents per acre. The Cash Sale Land Act was enforced until the general repeal of 1891.

The Act of March 3, 1807 forbade advance settlement of public lands prior to the sale, and provided for the punishment of trespassers. The Act of 1807 did not stop the trespassing on public lands. Therefore, between 1807 and 1841, several preemption laws were passed which gave squatters the right to purchase land (160 acres) upon which they had settled. Finally, in 1841, Congress passed the General Preemption Land Act, of September 4, 1841 (5 stat. 453), permitting settlers to enter surveyed or unsurveyed public lands and secure patent to the land after complying with the residence and cultivation requirements, and paid a minimum fee. The Preemption Act of 1841 was repealed in 1891.

145

Private Land Claims, patents, Act of December 22, 1854, (10 stat. 599), stipulated that any Spanish or Mexican Land Grant could be issued patent if, prior to Devember 22, 1854, the claimants could legally prove its existence as a bonafide grant.

TOWNSHIP GRID

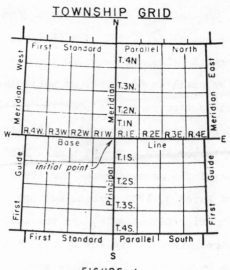

FIGURE 1

146

TOWNSHIPS

6	5	4	3	2	1
7	8	9	10	11	12
18	17	16	15	14	13
19	20	21	22	23	24
30	29	28	27	26	25
31	32	33	34	35	36

FIGURE 2

SECTION

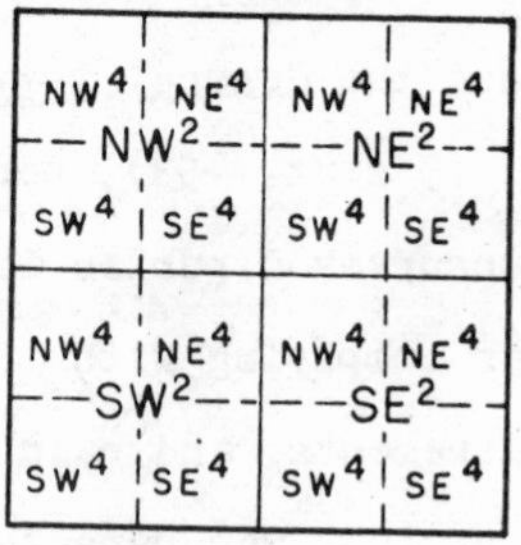

NW⁴ NW²	NE⁴	NW⁴ NE²	NE⁴
SW⁴	SE⁴	SW⁴	SE⁴
NW⁴ SW²	NE⁴	NW⁴ SE²	NE⁴
SW⁴	SE⁴	SW⁴	SE⁴

FIGURE 3

FROM MANUAL OF INSTRUCTIONS FOR THE SURVEY OF THE PUBLIC LANDS OF THE UNITED STATES, 1947, BUREAU OF LAND MANAGEMENT, UNITED STATES DEPARTMENT OF THE INTERIOR.

Frontier Donation Land Act came about through a
series of laws passed between 1842 and 1853. Land
donations were given settlers, who would act as armed
militia to protect settlements against Indian attacks.
Thus the Donation Land Act differed in purpose from the
Homestead Act. Furthermore, it applied only to certain
territories of the Public Domain: Florida, Oregon,
Washington and New Mexico.

By 1853, the Donation Act in New Mexico appears to
have been merely serving the function of rewarding early
settlers. Settlers were given 160 acres and required
to hold four years residence and attempt some sort of
cultivation. Grants under this act amounted to 20,105
acres in New Mexico; only 960 acres were in the claim
area.

147

The Five Year Homestead Act of May 20, 1862
(12 stat, 392) permitted settlers to enter a claim for a
maximum of 160 acres of either surveyed or unsurveyed
public lands. Settlers were entitled to a patent after
they had constructed a habitable house, cultivated part
of the claim and lived on the claim five years. There
was no charge for the land, except the land office
service charge. The act provided that title to the
claim could be secured before the five year period by
the minumum payment of one dollar and twenty-five cents
or two dollars and fifty cents an acre, but only after

the claim had been surveyed. Such a claim is listed as
a Cash Entry.

The Desert Land Act of March 3, 1877 (19 stat. 377)
applied to land that could not be cultivated without
irrigation. Its purpose was the development of arid and
semi-arid lands through irrigation. A claimant did not
have to live on the claim, but had to show that he could
profitably farm with the aid of irrigation. He also
paid a minimum of one dollar and twenty-five cents an
acre and could claim up to 320 acres.

The Timber Culture Act of June 14, 1878 (20 stat.
113) attempted to encourage timber culture on the prairies
by alloting land to those who would plant trees and protect
them. A settler, in addition to his homestead entry could
acquire, though it was not encouraged, 160 acres more
through the Timber Culture Act. Forty acres (later
ten acres) of the 160 acres were to be planted
in trees. The settler gained title after ten
(later eight) years. Within the period he could turn the
claim in as a cash entry by paying one dollar and twenty-
five cents an acre.

This act led to a new form of land speculation: the
sale of relinquishments. With a small amount of capital,
an individual could hold land for several years until the
number of settlers in the area had increased, then sell

148

his rights by relinquishment at a profit. A tract
of land might change hands repeatedly. If a settler
actually claimed the tract, he paid the speculator's
price before taking possession. New entries for certain
tracts were filed on the same dates as the relinquishments.

In Colorado, claimants held great tracts of land for
range purposes under this act. Sometimes it was a condition of employment that ranch hands make timber culture
entries for their employers. Such entries could be
held for an indefinite period of time through
relinquishment and refiling. Thus the act made
possible one development of large private land holdings,
especially in the plains area of Colorado.

The act was repealed on March 3, 1891 (26 stat. 1095).   149

Sale of Mineral Lands Acts of July 26, 1866 (14 stat.
252), July 9, 1870 (16 stat. 217), and May 10, 1872
17 stat. 91) provided that the discoverer of a mineral
deposit be given title to the discovery and that he should
receive patent to the claim upon payment of two dollars
and fifty cents per acre for a placer deposit or five
dollars for a lode deposit.

A special law was enacted for the Sale of Coal Lands,
March 3, 1873 (17 stat. 607). Coal claims were not to
exceed 160 acres per person or 640 acres per company.
minimum fee of ten dollars an acre was paid where deposit
were more than fifteen miles from a completed railroad,
r twenty dollars an acre where the deposit was less than
ifteen miles from the railroad.

The Homestead Act of 1862 and the Timber Culture Act of 1878 were the land acts most effective in stimulating settlement in the claim area.

NUMBER OF ACRES

No. of acres indicated the acreage per claim.

DATE OF ENTRY

Date of entry is the date upon which the claim was filed.

TRACTBOOK AND PAGE NUMBER

This sub-title for New Mexico was abandoned because sections were recorded according to range and township. Tract books were divided into sixteen townships each, e.g., Book 1, Range 1, Townships 1 to 16; Book 2, Range 1, Townships 17 to 32; Book 3, Range 2, Townships 1 to 16, and so forth.

150

DATE, PATENT OR PROVEN

This appears only on the Colorado data sheets.

DATE CANCELLED

Date cancelled appears only on the Colorado data sheets and refers either to the cancellation date of the claim, or to the date of relinquishment. It should be noted that a cancellation was made by the government, whereas relinquishment was a voluntary act by the claimant

Abbreviations used in claim entry data

Act. of Cong. - Act of Congress

Canc - Cancellation or cancelled

CE - Cash entry

Coal (not abbreviated)

DLE - Desert land entry

DC - Donation claim

EO - Executive Order

E - Entry

FC - Cinal certificate

HD, H, HE - Homestead entry

Lot - (not abbreviated)

ME - Mineral entry

Pat - Patent

Pre - Preemption

PLC - Private land claim

RR - Railroad

Ry - Railway

Rej - Rejected or rejection

Rel- relinquished or relinquishment

R W - right of way

Scrip Pat - Scrip Patent

Subdiv Und - Subdivisions undefined

Sus - suspended

term - terminate, termination

TC - Timber Culture

T or Tp - township

Tps - townships

War Dept.- War Department

Wt - Warrant

Wdl - withdrawal

Wdn - withdrawn

151

Literature Consulted

Bureau of Land Management. Manual of Instructions for the Survey of the Public Lands of the United States. Washington: 1928.

Bureau of Land Management. Manual of Surveying Instruction, 1947, Washington: 1947.

Department of the Interior. Manual of Surveying Instruction for the Survey of the Public Lands of the United States and Private Land Claims, 1 January 1890. Washington: 1890.

Proudfit, S. V., and Frank M. Johnson. "Historical Outline and The Rectangular System of Surveying," Public Land System of the United States. Washington: 1924.

Senzel, Irving. Brief Notes on the Public Domain. Washington: no date.

Westphall, Victor. The Public Domain in New Mexico 1854-1891. New Mexico Historical Review, Vol. XXXIII, No. 1.

New Mexico Tabulations

Entries in New Mexico represent a southerly extension of the major area of settlement, that is eastern Colorado. The entries were largely for an area in the present counties of Union, Colfax, Harding, Mora, and Quay.

In New Mexico, some of the better farming areas, for example, the Rio Grande, Pecos, and Canadian River valleys, had already been settled by Mexicans. And, some of the better grazing and agricultural land was already in private land grants.

153

New Mexican entries for the claim area do not begin until 1861, with the exception of one entry for 1854. There are few entries between 1861 and 1870. A number of cash entries were made between 1870 and 1872. There was little settlement between 1873-1878. Again, a number of cash entries were made in 1879.

The principal period of settlement, represented largely by homestead entries, began in 1881. The peak years for New Mexico were 1881-1883 and 1885.

In the tabulations by present-day counties, only total number of entries is considered - type of entry is not indicated here; nor whether proven or cancelled. Railroads, private land claims and military reservations are not included in the following tabulation.

The north eastern counties of Union, Colfax, and Harding had the greatest number of entries. Below is a list by county of the total entries between 1861 and 1887:

                    Union - 523
                    Colfax - 344
                    Harding-206
                    Guadalupe - 74
                    Taos - 5
154   Torrance - 18
                     San Miguel - 154
                     Santa Fe - 153
                    Quay - 139
                    Mora - 78

                    Total entries - 1694

Union County

Public Domain settlement in present-day Union County began in 1876; though it was not extensive until 1879. The major years of settlement were 1881 and 1885. Tabulations for Union County show that 38% of all entries (1876-1887) were made in 1881 and 16% in 1885, leaving 48% in the other years.

Between 1876 and 1887 3.4% (120 square miles or 77,006 acres[1]) of the total area of Union County (3817 square miles) had been claimed. Of this 23 square miles (14,558 acres) were cancelled.

Colfax County

Settlement in Colfax County reached a peak in 1885; settlement fell off somewhat in 1886, and rose again in 1887.

Tabulations showed a more even yearly distribution of settlement in Colfax than in other counties; 21% settlement in 1881; 22% in 1885 and 15% in 1887.

The present area of Colfax County, including the Maxwell Grant, is 3765 square miles. Of this, 76 square miles (51,000 acres) or two percent was claimed up to and including 1887. Thirty-seven square miles were cancelled.

Harding County

In Harding County no entries were listed between 1875 and 1880. In 1881 there were 31 entries. In 1882, the peak year, 80 entries were listed. Entries fell in 1883 to 23, and to 13 in 1884. There was a slight rise

155

---
[1] aerial measurements are approximate.

to 28 in 1885, and another low of two entries in 1886.
In 1887, entries rose to 11.

Entries before 1875 made up 8.2% of the total
county entries; in 1881, 15%; 1882, 39%; and 1885, 13%.

About 2.4% (52 square miles, 33,160 acres) of the
total land area of Harding (2136 square miles) was claimed
between 1861 and 1887; 29 square miles (18,724 acres)
were cancelled.

San Miguel County

The total number of entries for San Miguel between
1861 and 1887 was 154, with a peak of 25% in 1883 and
another of 17% in 1885.

About 0.77% (36 square miles, 23,129 acres) of the
total land area of San Miguel (4749 square miles) was
claimed; 29 square miles (18,491 acres) were cancelled.

Santa Fe County

There was some settlement in Santa Fe County before
1875 (46 entries), but very little between 1875 and 1886;
30% of the entries were made before 1875, 13% in 1883,
and 30% in 1887, leaving 27% for the remaining years.

Only 2.7% (33 square miles, 21,443 acres) of the
portion of Santa Fe County in the claim area (1205 square
miles) was claimed; 23 square miles (14,902 acres) were
cancelled.

Quay County

There were 139 listings for Quay County. There
was considerable settlement before 1815 (35.2%), but
none between 1875 and 1880. The peak year was 1883 with
31 entries (22.3%).

In the portion of the claim area in the county (2566 square miles) only 1.2% (32 square miles, 20,753 acres) was claimed in Quay. Four square miles (2,354 acres) were cancelled.

Mora County

There were 78 entries for Mora County between 1879 and 1887; 29% of the total entries were in 1882 and 22% in 1885.

0.92% (18 square miles, 11,372 acres) of Mora County was claimed (total area, 1942 square miles). Seven square miles (4,507 acres) were cancelled.

Guadalupe County

Though settlement in Guadalupe was low, it was steady with two peaks, in 1882 (31%) and 1885 (16%). 0.9% (19 square miles, 12,188 acres) was claimed in the claim area (1632 square miles) of Guadalupe. Twelve square miles (7,730 acres) were cancelled.

157

Torrance, Bernalillo and Taos Counties

Settlement in these counties was very slight: 18 entries for Torrance; nine for Bernalillo; and five for Taos.

Entries for the claim area (647 square miles) of Torrance included five square miles; four square miles (2721 acres) were cancelled.

Entries were made for two square miles (1436 acres) in the claim area (149.4 square miles) of Bernalillo.

Entries were made for only 800 acres in the claim area (1964 square miles) of Taos; all were cancelled.

Las Animas County

Las Animas County showed a more even settlement pattern. Settlement began in 1870 and between 1870 and 1880, 344 entries were made. The number of entries increased steadily to 1883; dropped off between 1884 and 1886; and rose again in 1887.

528 square miles (337,804 acres), or eleven percent of Las Animas County (4,794 square miles or 3,068,160 acres), were cancelled.

158

UNION (number of acres)

Patented			Cancelled
160-310	43	161.77	160-71
40-23	158.62	160.48	151.26
80-37	146.73	78.41	200
123.08	140.99	169.84	160.93
164.59	156.85	166.74	37.28
77.02.	32.14	119.86	73.92
161.92	153.44	158.96	158.18
164.42	71.96	82.74	159.91
163.19	156.12	121.08	158.54
160.48	158.27	85.70	167.48
155.95	141.52	158.88	164.46
118.55	34.39	140.13	156.12
77.76	154.81	22.47	80-2
39.89	40.43		162.03
159.81	39.38		122.89
156.26	159.06		40
116.73	159.		84.47
153.03	76.68		158.67
114.20	153.20		159.15
75.40	82.40		159.76
120.15	159.89		158.13
40.24	77.64		142.66
161.61	129.06		102.79
159.35	155.05		
167.20	49.21		

Total: 62,447.58   Total: 14,558.11

GRAND TOTAL
77,005.69 acres

HARDING (NUMBER OF ACRES)

Patented	Cancelled
160-65	160-102
40-5	80-5
120-10	120-6
320	149.70
200-2	200
77.72	160.97
195.49	157.10
280	320
143.14	40
80-4	104.14
159.47	151.84
81.58	160.34
165.99	
164.02	
167.50	
161.47	

Total: 14,436.38   Total: 18,724.09

GRAND TOTAL
33,160.47 acres

GUADALUPE (NUMBER OF ACRES)

Patented	Cancelled
160-19	160-28
120-2	160.57
80-3	80-6
200-2	133.16
207	120
40-2	40-2
91.79	200
159.65	640-2
	320
	635.87
Total: 4,458.44	Total 7,729.60

GRAND TOTAL
12,188.04 acres

RIO ARRIBA (NUMBER OF ACRES)

160

Patented	Cancelled
160-12	160-16
150.61	40-2
78.93	150-71
150.31	120
80-2	160.80
132.67	160.94
153.95	132.67
110.93	159.06
72.23	63.77
	63.97
Total: 2,929.71	Total: 3,651.92

GRAND TOTAL
6.581.63 acres

(number of acres)

Patented	Cancelled
	160-5
	Total: 800

COLFAX (number of acres)

Patented			Cancelled	
160-137	157.71	156.02	160.95	162.72
80.61	120-5	161.52	80-2	39.94
81.01	160.70	162.73	159.49	164.24
159.64	160.39		79.68	150.01
80-28	160.54		480	155.39
	165.13		136.71	39.30
				160.34
				320

COLFAX-continued

atented	Cancelled	
55.30	139.35	169.65
56.35	203.82	
52.56	163.18	
72.78	151.25	
0-11	38.94	
58.15	120-2	
60.90	40-3	
154.60	79.36	
56.30	326.07	
78.76	163.15	
59.66	560	
80.92	640-2	
77.58	600-3	
67.01	107.25	
1.60	136.42	
6.88	161.61	
64.24	162.01	
60.80	160.76	
otal: 27,430.39	Total: 23,570.00	

GRAND TOTAL:
51,000.39 acres

SAN MIGUEL (number of acres)

atented	Cancelled		161
60-21	160-80	146.80	
40-6	159.32	162.60	
39.44	80-3	136.47	
80-5	158.35	29.44	
20	159.38	160.01	
39.77	120	161.38	
80.35	162.01	132.64	
37.98	121.72	152.74	
60.54	124.82	160.42	
59.70	163.16	159.35	
	140.59	160.24	
	105.16	83.18	
	160.67	160.38	
	160.27	319.92	
	136	134.60	
	177.66	162.07	
	320	360	
otal: 4,637.78	Total: 18,491.36		

GRAND TOTAL
23,129.14 acres

SANTA FE (Number of Acres)

Patented		Cancelled
160-11	79.40	160-64
80-8	119.47	160.35
20.66-6	79.76	80-6
320	39.60	158.45
240	201.40	78.05
378.38	9.06	140.94
88.22	10.33-2	138.23
157.19	163.30	149.27
139.29	141.91	138.97
134.82		135.90
30.23		137.37
120.11		143.48
110.57		99.60
3.40		57.23
120-3		474.96
13.59		155.65
46.95		478.23
200		120
111.24		130.29
40-4		150.39
137.01		320.40
151		40
113,27		640
146.51		134.90
Total: 6,540.30		Total: 14,902.7

GRAND TOTAL:
21,443.06 acres

QUAY (number of acres)

Patented		Cancelled
160-41	335.03	
40-7	337.74	Cancelled
157.66	243.08	160-9
149.36	81.98	154.47
33.30	143.87	160.12
145.83	79.75	80-2
80-20	51.40	40
219.17	360.40	159.89
111.21	285.75	240
146.48	352.11	
120-6	506.34	
413.29	381.83	
25.80	212.09	
86.50	250.12	
136.49	125.32	
32.58	120.11	
61.58	82.71	

Quay-continued

Patented
88.49	80.28	Cancelled
279.70	118.23	
73.52	118.24	
200-5	120.55	
40.23	120.49	
160.44	80.42	
75.37	280	
80.64	320	
80.56	200.39	
292.92		

Total: 18,398.31   Total: 2,354.48

GRAND TOTAL:
20,752.79

MORA (number of Acres)

Patented	Cancelled
60-35	160-12
80-4	40
40-2	642.02
161.02	360
146.65	120-2
158.55	139.10
39.75	80
119.55	322.60
160.27	
79.42	
Total: 6,865.21	Total: 4,507.32

163

GRAND TOTAL:
11,372.53 acres

Torrence (number of acres)

Patented	Cancelled
160-2	160-11
159.12	80-2
40	640
Total: 519.12	Total: 272.36

GRAND TOTAL:
3,240.48

	HE Pat	Canc	Total	CE	TC Pat	Canc	Total	MISC Pat	Canc	Total	Grand Tot
Taos											
1884	3		3								3
1887	2		2								2
Union											
1876										4	4
1879		4	4	43							47
1880		4	4	37				1	2	3	44
1881	110	8	118	83							201
1882	14	15	29	12							41
1883	25	8	33	4					1	1	38
1884	10		10	1							11
1885	53	12	65	31							96
1886	1	4	5		1		1				6
1887		9	9	3		21	21	1	1	2	35
Colfax											
1876			1								1
1879		4	4	19							23
1880		2	2	34				1		1	37
1881	28	15	43	27					1	1	71
1882	5	17	22	18					2	2	42
1883	6	8	14	5					2	2	21
1884		6	6	3	1		1				10
1885	52	17	69	4	1		1		2	2	76
1886		6	6		1		1		3	3	10
1887		12	12	9	27		27		5	5	53

164

	HE			CE	TC			MISC			
Year	Pat	Canc	Total	Pat	Pat	Canc	Total	Pat	Canc	Total	Grand Total

Harding County

Year	HE Pat	HE Canc	HE Total	CE Pat	TC Pat	TC Canc	TC Total	MISC Pat	MISC Canc	MISC Total	Grand Total
1861		1	1								1
1872				16							16
1880		1	1								1
1881	16	15	31								31
1882	10	69	79	1							80
1883	18	5	23								23
1884	5	7	12			1	1				13
1885	20	5	25	3							28
1886		1	1			1	1				2
1887		1	1	1	1	8	9				11

Quay County

Year	HE Pat	HE Canc	HE Total	CE Pat	TC Pat	TC Canc	TC Total	MISC Pat	MISC Canc	MISC Total	Grand Total
1871				11							11
1872				38							38
1881	1		1								1
1882	22	3	25			2	2		2	2	29
1883	31		31								31
1884	2	3	5								5
1885	18	1	19						1	1	20
1886						1	1				1
1887	1	2	3								3

166

	HE			CE		TC	MISC			Grand Total
	Pat	Canc	Total	Pat	Canc	Total	Pat	Canc	Total	
San Miguel County										
1870		1	1							1
1872				1						1
1875	1		1							1
1876		1	1		1	1				2
1877		1	1		1	1				1
1880	1		1							1
1881		16	16							16
1882	8	20	28							28
1883	5	29	34	1				3	3	38
1884	12	4	16							16
1885	10	12	22		3	3		1	1	26
1886		3	3							3
1887		15	15		4	4		1	1	20
Santa Fe County										
1869		1	1							1
1870		1	1	13 (1 canc)						15
1871		3	3	23						26
1872				3						3
1874								1	1	1
1875				2						2
1880	1		1			2			2	3
1881								1	1	1
1882		6	6							6

	HE			CL	TC			MISC			Grand Total
	Pat	Canc	Total		Pat	Canc	Total	Pat	Canc	Total	
Santa Fe County - cont'd											
1883	2	12	14			2	2	4		4	20
1884		1	1								1
1885	5	5	10	2							12
1886		4	4			10	10	1	1	2	16
1887		8	8	2		24	24	3	9	12	46
Rio Arriba											
1883		10	10								10
1884		1	1								1
1885	19	11	30								30
1887		1	1								1
Torrence											
1883		1	1								1
1885	1		1	1							2
1886		1	1						1	1	2
1887	1	2	3	1		6	6		3	3	13
Bernalillo											
1881		1	1								1
1882	3		3								3
1883		1	1								1
1885	1		1								1
1887		2	2						1	1	3

167

	HE			CE	TC			MISC			Grand Total
	Pat	Canc	Total		Pat	Canc	Total	Pat	Canc	Total	
Mora											
1881	2	4	6	2							8
1882	10	6	16	7							23
1883	13	1	14								14
1885	14	3	17								17
1886		4	4					1		1	5
1887		9	9					2		2	11
Guadalupe											
1867		1	1								1
1872				6							6
1873				1							1
1876	2	2	4			2	2				6
1878	1		1			2	2	1		1	4
1882	6	11	17			3	3		3	3	23
1883	2	8	10								10
1884		1	1		1					1	2
1885	10	1	11						1	1	12
1886									1	1	1
1887		3	3	1		3	3		1	1	8

168

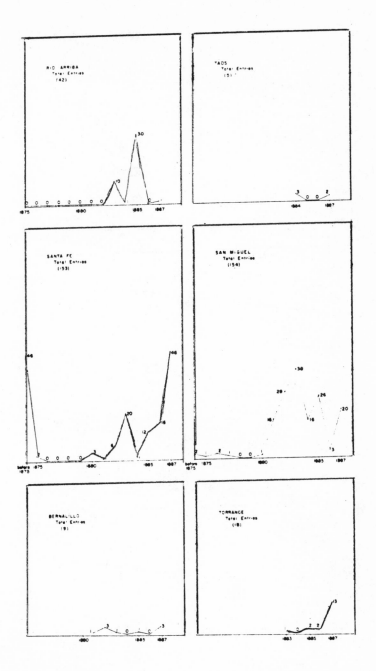

169

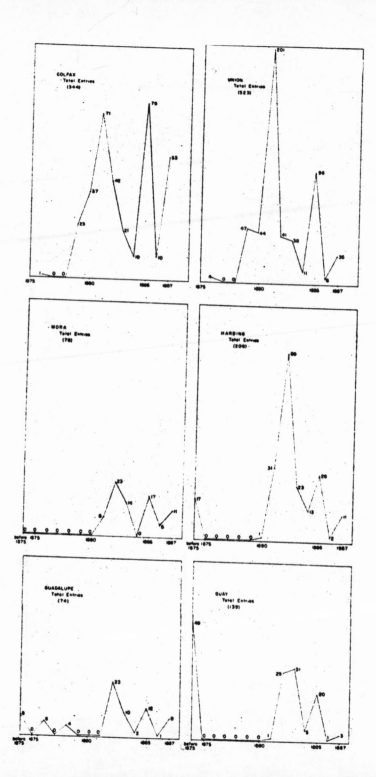

Colorado Tabulations

Tabulations for Colorado were based on present county boundaries; tabulations were made only for county areas south of the Arkansas River and east of the Rocky Mountains.

Settlement under the landacts began in southeastern Colorado in 1865, particularly in Baca, Prowers, Las Animas, Pueblo and Bent counties. Less interest was shown by the settlers in Huerfano, Otero, Custer and Fremont Counties.

In general, the years 1886 and 1887 had the greatest number of entries:

	Homestead		Timber Culture	
	Patented	Cancelled	Patented	Cancelled
1886	166	79	117	1214
1887	391	1430	121	3271

171

15,110 entries were listed for the years 1861 to, and including 1887:

Baca — 3642

Prowers - 2510

Las Animas - 2231

Bent - 1167

Pueblo - 2231

Huerfano - 953

Otero - 931

Custer - 749

Fremont - 696

LAS ANIMAS COUNTY

Cancelled

160.00-587	154.52-2	159.77	160.98
80.00-22	160.53	154.68	160.16
160.44	161.08	166.69	160.57
160.59-2	160.37	166.89	159.93
165.57	157.25	165.05	170.25
164.07	167.09	161.57	160.56-2
160.97	167.75	160.60	166.65
160.62	159.24	160.40	160.69
159.92-2	160.10	159.88	160.32
160.47	161.26	163.82	160.81
160.27	160.79	160.13	161.27
160.25-2	161.13	179.20	161.17
137.40	142.86	158.17	146.01
161.03	156.76	171.70	161.49
120.00-2	151.97	169.95	160.06
85.00	161.04	170.74	160.35
158.75	130.30	159.40	157.50
160.39	158.35	119.88	159.03
158.92	177.07	160.75	181.23
166.48	168.34	120.35	91.40
160.86	154.96	40.00-5	147.61-2
158.96	156.96-2	159.02	85.85
135.41	166.13	158.31	157.84
148.31	157.56	160.43	159.95

172

Total:
113,448.04

LAS ANIMAS COUNTY

Patented

160.00-1060	162.92	80.00-67	164.41
40.00-28	159.59	120.00-54	160.14
159.26	165.21	162.19	160.26
166.89	159.93	160.19	160.32
157.31	160.10	163.19	160.50
171.80	167.51	11.80	161.12
108.22	174.80	168.51	162.09
170.45	160.55	171.40	175.04
159.88	160.32	39.21	185.67
156.90	142.24	124.56	103.34
80.60	153.22	148.63	171.24
132.95	160.06	121.86	159.93
78.81	161.93	156.00	159.51
156.29	155.01	160.20	160.45
157.91	156.51	50.30	160.11
135.20	80.90	165.56	160.12
147.68	160.39	130.30	161.08
159.72	159.32	148.81	154.80
159.55	156.68	158.82-2	157.39

continued

LAS ANIMAS COUNTY

Patented-continued

160.06	160.75	161.04	10.23	152.55
135.86	148.35	160.34	10.33	155.22
154.41	6.90	135.41	166.14	165.61
159.88	168.54	154.06	164.41	149.54
171.20	153.09	153.00	158.75	160.05
158.50	158.92-2	155.71	155.89	135.39
162.18	157.66	149.28	166.00	156.50
160.78	158.56	153.52	163.43	159.61
160.56	156.64	119.94	160.38	162.15
157.81	159.09	157.34	160.14	171.46
158.21	159.19	40.80	157.04	170.91
154.34	165.60	8.01	160.02	129.16
153.82	161.24	168.01	159.88	160.61
160.20	84.69	105.06	160.40	163.00
159.39	153.63	154.54	79.83	160.82
162.10	38.80-2	146.16	159.77	162.46
160.09	156.52	141.14	159.55	143.15
160.07	157.86	69.36	79.34	142.73
164.52	156.60	153.25	160.09	140.54
267.93	157.80	156.84	77.16	141.86
161.50	157.30	36.84	159.72	144.35
160.28	155.10	154.10	159.82	134.44
160.39	156.04	154.98	159.80	168.18
160.74	154.68	34.93	158.22	159.69
160.60	150.29	12.00-2	119.27	162.71
160.16	153.11	76.97	160.39-2	164.80
153.00	117.91	78.99	160.32	
157.90	111.66	159.05	159.93	
88.86	320.00	157.15-2	170.24	
157.48	159.48	156.97	175.09	
117.76	159.13	158.51	123.82	
67.00	160.41	169.77	85.05	
77.05	159.07	154.68	165.09	
110.32	161.74	159.54	85.00	
156.23	161.64	159.62	158.65	
155.34	151.04	80.09	167.73	
160.14	170.18	168.25	172.71	
154.93	161.81	175.97	160.88	
159.81	152.53	175.93	157.24	
78.16	161.47	160.29	80.52	
78.14	158.27	159.88	79.13	
116.52	157.59	80.77	160.54	
156.83	158.62	161.04	159.35	
157.23	157.52	160.34	162.33	
156.55	155.92	159.67	160.62	
156.40	153.66	159.85	161.56	

173

Total:
224,355.94
GRAND TOTAL:
337,803.98

		HE			CE	TC			MISC			Grand Total
		Pat	Canc	Total		Pat	Canc	Total	Pat	Canc	Total	

Las Animas

Year	Pat	Canc	Total	CE	Pat	Canc	Total	Pat	Canc	Total	Grand Total
1870	6	1	7						3	3	10
1873	142	10	152	1							153
1874	23	1	24						1	1	25
1875	48	2	50		12	1	13				63
1876	31	2	33	2	1	1	2	3		3	40
1877	15	8	23			1		1		1	25
1878	40	9	40					9		9	50
1879	39	17	56	4							60
1880	103	3	106	1				1		1	108
1881	122	14	136					13	1	14	150
1882	164	24	188	7		1		9		9	205
1883	317	49	366	12	2	4	6	31	1	32	416
1884	108	24	132	6	1	9	10	5		5	153
1885	77	31	108	12	1	6	7	3	7	10	137
1886	44	21	65	8	2	17	19		1	1	93
1887	51	105	156	14	8	346	326	19		19	543

174

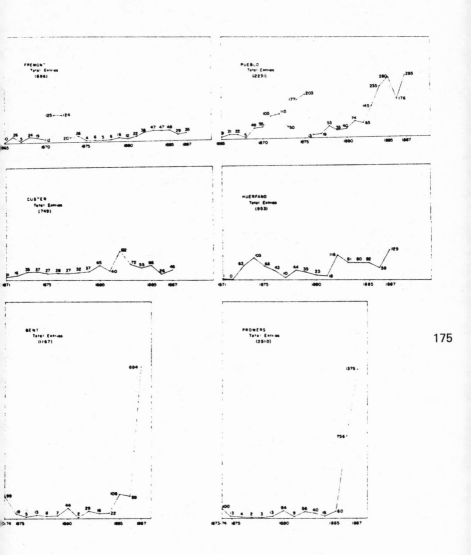

175

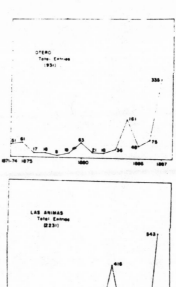

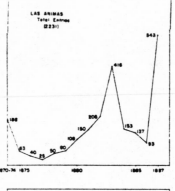

APPENDIX TWO: RECORDED SALES OF LAND
AND LAND VALUE (SUMMARY)

Deeds of sale are recorded at the courthouses
in the county seats within the claim area. At some
county seats the records extend back to the period
of interest in this study, namely 1847 to 1887.
Representatives of the Jicarilla Apache Tribal Claim
Committee and the University of New Mexico Geography
Department travelled to these county seats during
the summers of 1960 and 1961. Deeds pertinent to
the period 1847 to 1887 were studied and a very large
amount of information on land sales collected. In
particular, the following information was noted:

(1) The name of the county seat
(2) The number and page of the book in which
     the deed is recorded
(3) The date of the sale
(4) A description of the location and bound-
     aries of the sold land
(5) The acreage of the tract sold, if indicated
(6) The sale price

It is impossible to include here all of the
information gathered; it is on file at the UNM Geography Department. Summary tabulations of interest in

considering the value of land in the claim area is
presented at the end of this appendix. More than
thirteen hundred transactions are included. The
table shows the years of sales, the number of sales
and the average prices per acre.

The table includes only properties described
according to the U. S. General Land Office system
(i.e. according to township, range, section, etc.).
All sales are of tracts of over forty acres; more
than 90 per cent of the sales listed are for tracts
of 160 acres or more. Sales in which other property
than land (e.g. cattle and equipment) was included
have not been listed in the tabulations.

178

For the first half of the period 1847 to 1887,
many deeds are written in Spanish. Pertinent pass-
ages in these deeds have been copied and translated.
Here also, sales have been included in the tabulations only where the land was described according to
the U. S. Land Office system. Other sales recorded
in Spanish are not included. For a number of reasons
they are difficult to interpret for purposes of deter-
mining land value. Economy before the arrival of
Americans was partly on a barter basis; full cash
value was seldom paid for land. Before the initiation
of the U. S. Land Office surveys, boundaries were
seldom described in such a way that the acreage of a

property can be accurately determined. For example, a tract is often described as extending a certain number of _varas_ along a stream course; the extent of the land away from the stream course is usually not specified. Markers were often impermanent; a property might, for instance, be described as extending from a "cottonwood grove to a neighbor's corral."

Sales of land within the land grants are not included in the tabulations; thus on the map there are large unstippled areas outlined by the Sangre de Cristo Grant in Costilla County, the Tierra Amarilla Grant in Rio Arriba County, the Maxwell Grant in western Colfax County, the Canyon de San Diego Grant in the Jemez Mountains, the Mora Grant in Mora County the Pablo Montoya Grant in San Miguel County, and others.

179

Mexican farmers and ranchers owned much of the good land in the Rio Grande Valley when the surveys of the U. S. General Land Office were made. Thus, as indicated on the map, few sales of land described according to the Land Office system are recorded in counties of dense Mexican settlement.

New Mexican counties like Guadalupe, Quay, Union and Harding were formed after 1887; thus their court-houses have no pertinent records.

In the tables the sales are segregated according
to the county seat in which the deeds are recorded.
Because the history of change in county areas is very
complex, the map has been drawn to show the actual
distribution of the land sold, within the grid of
the U. S. General Land Office.

180

Year	No. of Entries	Average price per acre	year	No. of entries	Average price per acre
		Las Animas County			
1868	2	15.37	1878	5	8.54
1870	1	9.38	1879	2	7.52
1873	37	5.35	1880	1	1.88
1874	35	4.46	1881	7	2.61
1875	26	4.83	1882	19	3.40
1876	9	6.04	1883	42	6.13
1877	5	3.27	1888	6	10.65

Year	No. of entries	Average price per acre	Year	No. of entries	Average price per acre
		Santa Fe County			
1871	2	.83	1875	1	2.56
1872	1	1.25	1885	4	1.55
1873	2	5.00	1886	2	2.00
1874	1	2.20	1887	17	20.20
		Mora County			
1880	3	1.51	1884	20	6.38
1881	50	1.41	1885	27	4.92
1882	39	4.15	1886	10	5.79
1883	26	4.38	1887	14	6.95
		Colfax County			
1869	1	3.90	1880	92	2.98
1870	1	3.13	1881	52	6.49
1871	1	12.25	1882	64	4.55
1875	5	3.28	1883	57	4.68
1876	2	2.51	1884	22	3.96
1877	2	2.19	1885	4	3.44
1878	3	3.12	1886	2	2.95
1879	51	2.33	1887	1	3.15
		San Miguel County			
1878	1	1.63	1884	18	5.89
1881	1	7.50	1885	36	6.02
1882	107	4.96	1886	31	4.24
1883	70	2.29	1887	2	16.87

181

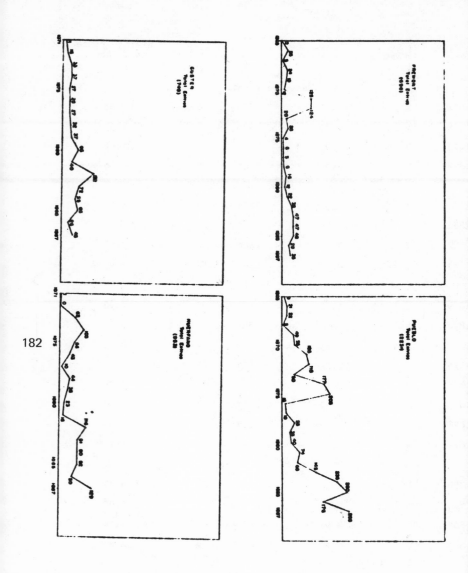

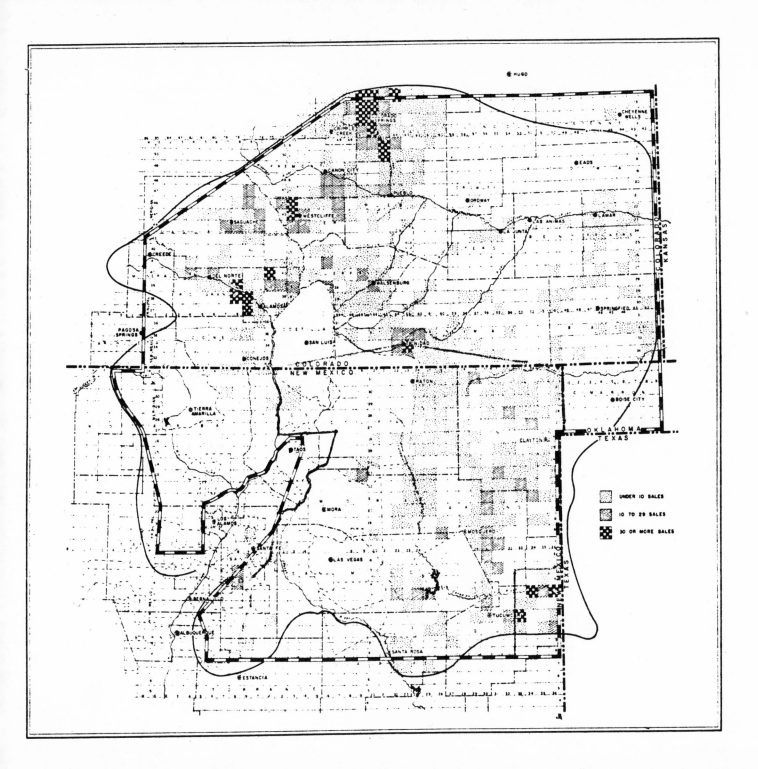

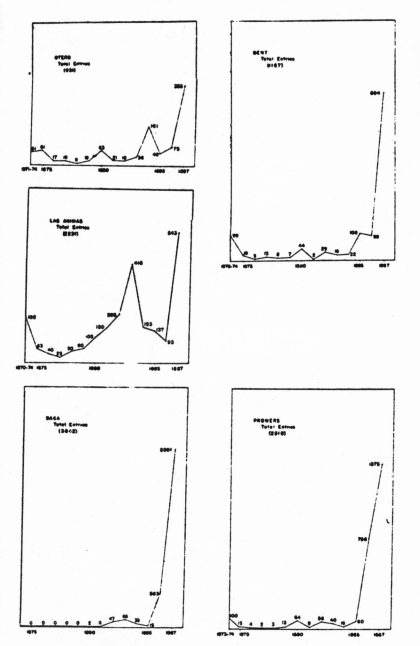

183

184

APPENDIX THREE: RECORDED SALES OF LAND
AND LAND VALUE (DETAILS)

The following tabulation lists sales of land described
according to the U. S. General Land Office system. The number of
the deed book and the page number upon which the sale is recorded
are on file at the Geography Department, University of New Mexico.

Small parcels of land, sold during the period of interest here,
were mainly around the larger towns and these small tracts are the
ones which changed hands frequently. Since sales of such small
tracts are not tabulated here, the list includes a few resales.

At the end of the tabulation is a list of sales within land
grants. However, the list is not complete. Those sales which
include the barter of other property than land (cattle, farm
equipment, etc.) or sales of parts of grants (the part not being
specified) are not listed.

185

In many of the deeds recorded in Spanish, it is now impossible
to determine the boundaries and extent of the land sold. Sample
copies of deeds recorded in Spanish are given at the end of the
tabulations.

Claimant's Exhibit No. PLG-2
Docket 22A

SANTA FE COUNTY

Year	Township	Range	Section	Parts of Sections	No. of Acres	Sales Price
1871	14N	8E	18	NE¼	800	500
			7	E½ of NE¼		
				SE¼		
			8	NW¼		
				SW¼		
			17	W½ of NW¼		
1872	14N	8E	8	½ of NE¼	80	100

186

COLFAX COUNTY

Year	Township	Range	Section	Parts of Sections	No. of Acres	Sales Price
1870	29N	25E	7 6	Part Part	160	500
1875	27N	25E	34	E½ of NE¼	80	200
1875	26N	24E	15 22	S½ of SE¼ NW¼ of NE¼	120	200
1878	31N	31_	17 20	E¼ of SW¼ S½ of SE¼ NW¼ of NE¼	160	300
1878	29N	27E	15	NE¼ of NW¼ W½ of NE¼ SE¼ of NE¼	160	500
1878	25N	27E	23 14	W½ of NE¼ NE¼ of NW¼ SE¼ of SW¼	160	300
1878	26N	28E	23 26	S½ of SW¼ W½ of NW¼	160	500
1878	25N	28E	20 29	W½ of SE¼ NW¼ of NE¼ NE¼ of NW¼	160	350
1878	25N	27E	25 24	E½ of SW¼ NW¼ of NW¼ SW¼ of SW¼	160	300
1878	25N	28E	8 17	SW¼ of SE¼ W½ of NE¼ NW¼ of SE¼	160	300
1878	25N	28E	30	SE¼ of NW¼ NE¼ of SW¼ SW¼ of NE¼ NW¼ of SE¼	160	400
1878	25N	28E	32	W½ of NE¼ S½ of NW¼	160	500
1878	31N	30E	13	S½ of NE¼ NE¼ of SW¼ SE¼ of NW¼	160	350
1878	31N	30E	22 23	NE¼ of NE¼ N½ of NE¼ NW¼ of NW¼		

187

Year	Township	Range	Section	Parts of Sections	No. of Acres	Sales Price
1878	31N	30E	23 14 13	NE¼ of NE¼ SE¼ of SE¼ W½ of SW¼	160	390
1878	31N	31E	18	NW¼ of SW¼ S½ of NW¼ SW¼ of NE¼	170	375
1878	31N	31E	14 23	NE¼ of SW¼ SW¼ of SE¼ NE¼ of NW¼	120	350
1878	31N	31E	13	NE¼ of NW¼ W½ of NE¼ NE¼ of NE¼	160	350
1878	31N	31E	14	NE¼ of SW¼ NW¼ of SE¼ S½ of SE¼	160	350
1878	25N	28E	32 33	SE¼ of NE¼ SW¼ of NW¼	80	1,000
1878	31N	31E	13 14	SW¼ of NW¼ N½ of SW¼ NE¼ of SE¼	160	300
1878	25N	28E	19 30	E½ of SW¼ NE¼ of NW¼ NW¼ of NE¼	160	300
1878	25N	28E	18 19	E½ of SW¼ E½ of NW¼	160	325
1879	30N	24E	25 26	Part Part	160	300
1879	32N	33E	30	SE¼ of NW¼ W½ of NE¼ NE¼ of NE¼	160	400
1879	30N	30E	11	E½ of NE¼ E½ of SE¼	160	300
1879	28N	30E	1 2	NW¼ of SW¼ N½ of SE¼ NE¼ of SW¼	160	400
1879	31N	29E	22 21 28	Part Part Part	966	4,000

188

Year	Township	Range	Section	Parts of Sections	No. of Acres	Sales Price
1879	31N	29E	23	NW¼ of NW¼ S½ of NW¼ NW¼ of SW¼	160	100
1879	32N	27E	20 29	W½ of SW¼ SE¼ of SW¼ NE¼ of NW¼	162	450
1879	32N	27E	29	N½ of SE¼ SW¼ of NE¼ SE¼ of NW¼	160	400
1879	30N	25E	33 34	E½ of NE¼ of SE¼ SE¼ of NE¼ SW¼ of NW¼ NW¼ of SW¼	130	500
1879	32N	27E	19	N½ of SE¼ SE¼ of SE¼ NE¼ of SW¼	162	500
1879	32N	27E	33	W½ of SW¼ W½ of NW¼	160	500
1879	31N	31E	18 17	SE¼ of NE¼ E½ of SE¼ SW¼ of SW¼	160	300
1879	30N	25E	32 33	Part Part	160	300
1879	24N 22N	29E	31 6	W½ of SW¼ SE¼ of SW¼ NE¼ of NW¼	160	300
1879	29N	31E	16 21	W½ of SE¼ NW¼ of NE¼ NE¼ of NW¼	160	350
1879	29N	31E	16 15	E½ of NE¼ N½ of NW¼	160	150
1879	29N	24E	28 27	E½ of NE¼ NE¼ of SE¼ NW¼ of SW¼	160	500
1879	29N	31E	20 21	S½ of SE¼ NE¼ of SE¼ NW¼ of SW¼	160	290
1879	29N	30E	14 23	W½ of SE¼ W½ of NE¼	160	400

189

Year	Township	Range	Section	Parts of Sections	No. of Acres	Sales Price
1879	29N	30E	24 25	SW¼ of SE¼ N½ of NE¼	120	500
1879	29N	30E	30	W½ of NW¼ SE¼ of NW¼ SW¼ of NE¼	155	375
1879	29N	30E	15 14	SE¼ of SE¼ W½ of SW¼ NE¼ of SE¼	160	375
1879	29N	30E	14 23 24	E½ of SE¼ NE¼ of NE¼ NW¼ of NW¼	160	400
1879	29N	30E	24	S½ of NW¼ N½ of SW¼	160	500
1879	29N	30E	27 28	SW¼ of SW¼ S½ of SE¼ NW¼ of SE¼	160	380
1879	29N	30E	28 26	SE¼ of SW¼ NE¼ of NW¼ N½ of NE¼	160	350
1879	24N	28E	10	SE¼ of NW¼ E½ of SW¼ SW¼ of SE¼	160	290
1879	24N	28E	4 3 10	SE¼ of SE¼ SW¼ of SW¼ W½ of NW¼	160	340
1879	24N	28E	4	SE¼ of NW¼ SW¼ of NE¼ N½ of SE¼	160	300
1879	26N	29E	2 1	NE¼ of SE¼ N½ of SW¼ SW¼ of NW¼	160	300
1879	25N	24E	25 24	N½ of NW¼ NW¼ of NE¼ SE¼ of SW¼	160	1,000
1879	29N	31E	26 35 36 26 35 36	E½ of SE¼ NE¼ of NE¼ NW¼ of NW¼	160	300

190

Year	Township	Range	Section	Parts of Sections	No. of Acres	Sales Price
1879	24N	28E	14	N½ of SW¼ SE¼ of SW¼ SW¼ of SE¼	160	300
1879	24N	28E	15	W½ of NE¼ SE¼ of NE¼ NE¼ of SE¼	160	300
1879	24N	28E	23 24 25	SE¼ of SE¼ S½ of SW¼ NE¼ of NW¼	160	350
1879	24N	28E	23	N½ of NE¼ SE¼ of NE¼ NE¼ of SE¼	160	300
1879	24N	28E 29E	25 36 31	SE¼ of SE¼ NE¼ of NE¼ W½ of NW¼	160	300
1879	24N	28E	25	SE¼ of NW¼ SW¼ of NE¼ N½ of SE¼	160	300
1879	30N	24E	13	Part	80	200
1879	31N	32E	8	NW¼ of NE¼ NE¼ of NW¼ S½ of NW¼	160	350
1879	31N	32E	7 18	NE¼ of SW¼ S½ of SW¼ NW¼ of NW¼	160	500
1879	32N	34E	34	S½ of NW¼ N½ of SW¼	160	400
1880	29N	24E	27 28	NW¼ of SW¼ NE¼ of SE¼ E½ of NE¼	160	1,000
1880	27N	34E	11	S½ of NW¼ NE¼ of SW¼ NW¼ of SE¼	160	350
1880	29N	30E	15 14	SE¼ of SE¼ W½ of SW¼ NE¼ of SE¼	160	500
1880	26N	29E 30E	1 12 7	S½ of SE¼ NE¼ of NE¼ NW¼ of NW¼	160	275

191

Year	Township	Range	Section	Parts of Sections	No. of Acres	Sales Price
1880	30,31N	27E	2 3 34	NW¼ of NW¼ NE¼ of NE¼ S½ of SE¼	161	300
1880	29N	33E	22	W½ of SE¼ NE¼ of SW¼ SE¼ of NW¼	160	500
1880	31N	32E	9 4	NE¼ of NW¼ NW¼ of NE¼ S½ of SE¼	160	350
1880	26N	35E	9 16	E½ of SW¼ N½ of NW¼	160	300
1880	31N	32E	3	SE¼ of NE¼ N½ of SE¼ NE¼ of SW¼	160	400
1880	27N	34E	5 8	S½ of SW¼ N½ of NW¼	160	300
1880	27N	34E	3 10 11	E½ of SE¼ NE¼ of NE¼ NW¼ of NW¼	160	300
1880	23N	19E	12 11	Part Part	160	125
1880	26N	34E	9	E½ of NE¼ E½ of SE¼	160	300
1880	29N	24E	27	E½ of SW¼ NW¼ of SE¼ SW¼ of NE¼	160	1,000
1880	28N	32E	11 12	SE¼ of NW¼ S½ of NE¼ SW¼ of NW¼	160	400
1880	27N	34E	9 16 15	SE¼ of SE¼ E½ of NE¼ SW¼ of NW¼	160	350
1880	27N	34E	11 14	SW¼ of SE¼ W½ of NE¼ SE¼ of NE¼	160	400
1880	25N	24E 25E	25 24 19	NE¼ of NE¼ S½ of SE¼ SW¼ of SW¼	160	1,000

Year	Township	Range	Section	Parts of Sections	No. of Acres	Sales Price
1880	25N	31E	2	W½ of SE¼ E½ of SW¼	160	500
1880	25N	31E	12 11 2	NW¼ of NW¼ N½ of NE¼ SE¼ of SE¼	160	500
1880	29N	24E	25 26	NW¼ of SW¼ N½ of SE¼ SW¼ of SE¼	160	925
1880	29N	24E	27 26	SE¼ of NE¼ NE¼ of SE¼ N½ of SW¼	160	400
1880	29N	31E	14	N½ of NW¼ SE¼ of NW¼ NE¼ of SW¼	160	300
1880	26N	35E	7	N½ of SW¼ SE¼ of SW¼ SW¼ of SE¼	160	400
1880	29N	31E	13 18	SE¼ of NE¼ S½ of NW¼ SW¼ of NE¼	160	375
1880	27N	34E	11 14 13	SE¼ of SE¼ NE¼ of NE¼ W½ of NW¼	160	400
1880	25N	34E	33 32 5	SW¼ of SW¼ SE¼ of SE¼ N½ of NE¼	160	350
1880	27N	34E	9	W½ of NE¼ SE¼ of NW¼	120	350
1880	27N	34E	9	SE¼ of NW¼ NW¼ of NE¼ NE¼ of SW¼ W½ of SE¼	200	400
1880	29N	27E	10	E½ of SW¼ W½ of SE¼	160	1,000
1880	26N	25E 24E	17 24 13	N½ of SW¼ W½ of NW¼ NE¼ of NW¼ SE¼ of SW¼	240	2,000

193

Year	Township	Range	Section	Parts of Sections	No. of Acres	Sales Price
1880	27N	25E	34	E½ of NE¼	200	500
			15	S½ of SE¼		
	26N	24E	22	NW¼ of NE¼		
1880	30N	25E	26	S½ of SE¼	160	500
			35	N½ of NE¼		
1880	30N	25E	34	SE¼ of NW¼	160	500
				NW¼ of SW¼		
				S½ of SW¼		
1880	32N	33E	29	N½ of NW¼	160	300
				SE¼ of NW¼		
				SW¼ of NE¼		
1880	32N	33E	21	N½ of SE¼	160	400
			22	N½ of SW¼		
1880	31N	32E	2	W½ of NW¼	160	250
				NE¼ of NW¼		
	32N		35	SE¼ of SW¼		
1880	28N	31E	11	W½ of SW¼	160	300
			10	E½ of SE¼		
1880	27N	33E	2	NE¼ of SE¼	160	300
				N½ of SW¼		
			1	NW¼ of SE¼		
1880	29N	27E	11	SW¼	160	1,000
1880	25N	27E	15	N½ of NW¼	160	400
				N½ of NE¼		
1880	30N	34E	15	Part	160	350
			14	Part		
1880	30N	34E	29	Part	160	300
1880	29N	34E	17	Part	160	400
1880	29N	33E	14	Part	160	350
			13	Part		
1880	23N	29E	16	Part	160	400
1880	30N	33E	24	Part	160	400
1880	27N	33E	5	S½ of SW¼	160	300
				S½ of SE¼		

194

Year	Township	Range	Section	Parts of Sections	No. of Acres	Sales Price
1880	26N	25E	13	E½ of NE¼ SW¼ of NE¼ NW¼ of SE¼	160	400
1880	27N	32E	26 27 34 35	SW¼ of SW¼ SE¼ of SE¼ NW¼ of NE¼ NW¼ of NW¼	160	400
1880	27N	26E	7 18	SW¼ of SW¼ N½ of NW¼ SW¼ of NW¼	160	400
1880	27N	34E	14	Part	160	400
1880	27N	26E	6 7	S½ of SW¼ SW¼ of SE¼ NW¼ of NE¼	160	400
1880	29N	33E	15	Part	160	300
1880	29N	32E	15 22	Part Part	160	300
1880	29N	33E	16 17	Part Part	160	250
1880	29N	33E	21 22	Part Part	160	300
1880	27N	26E	23 24 25 26	SE¼ of SE¼ SW¼ of SW¼ NW¼ of NW¼ NE¼ of NE¼	160	400
1880	28N	33E	5 4	SE¼ of NE¼ S½ of NW¼ SW¼ of NE¼	160	400
1880	29N	24E	25	NE¼ of SW¼ W½ of SE¼ SE¼ of SE¼	160	1,000
1880	25N	26E	3 10	NW¼ of SE¼ S½ of SE¼ NE¼ of NE¼	160	400
1880	27N	26E	32	N½ of NE¼ E½ of NE¼	160	300

Year	Township	Range	Section	Parts of Sections	No. of Acres	Sales Price
1880	27N	26E	27 28	SW¼ of NW¼ S½ of NE¼ NE¼ of SE¼	160	500
1880	28N	32E	22 21	N½ of NW¼ SW¼ of NW¼ SE¼ of NE¼	160	400
1880	28N	32E	4	E½ of SW¼ W½ of SE¼	160	1,000
1880	28N	32E	12 1	N½ of NW¼ SE¼ of SW¼ SW¼ of SE¼	160	400
1880	27N	26E	35 36	SE¼ of NE¼ N½ of NE¼ NW¼ of NW¼	160	400
1880	29N	27E	10	N½ of NW¼	80	1,000
1880	30N	27E	33	E½ of NW¼ E½ of SW¼	160	250
1880	32N	32E	25	NE¼ of NE¼ W½ of SE¼ SW¼ of NE¼	160	350
1880	32N	35E	30 29	N½ of SE¼ NW¼ of SW¼ SW¼ of NW¼	160	475
1880	32N	33E	35	N½ of NW¼ W½ of NE¼	160	490
1880	30N	33E	23 24	S½ of SE¼ S½ of SW¼	160	350
1880	26N	25E	12 13	S½ of SW¼ SW¼ of SE¼ NW¼ of NE¼	160	2,000
1880	31N	33E	16	W½ of NW¼ W½ of SW¼	160	200
1880	29N	33E	25 26	W½ of NW¼ N½ of NE¼	160	400
1880	29N	33E	35	E½ of SW¼ SW¼ of SW¼	120	300

196

Year	Township	Range	Section	Parts of Sections	No. of Acres	Sales Price
1880	27N	25E	12 7	SE¼ of NE¼ NE¼ of NE¼ NW¼ of SW¼ SW¼ of NW¼	160	400
1880	27N	33E	3	S½ of SW¼ S½ of SE¼	160	400
1880	28N	31E	12 11	SW¼ of SW¼ S½ of SE¼ SE¼ of SW¼	160	350
1880	26N	25E	12 11 14	NW¼ of SW¼ E½ of SE¼ NE¼ of NE¼	160	500
1880	32N	33E	27 26	N½ of SE¼ SE¼ of SE¼ SW¼ of SW¼	160	500
1880	27N	33E	2	S½ of SW¼ W½ of SE¼	160	350
1880	29N	34E	32 31	N½ of NW¼ E½ of NE¼	160	400
1880	26N	35E	17 16	N½ of SE¼ SE¼ of SE¼ NW¼ of SE¼	160	400
1880	26N	35E	10 15	SE¼ of SW¼ SW¼ of SE¼ NE¼ of NW¼ NW¼ of NE¼	160	350
1880	29N	32E	22 27	W½ of SE¼ NW¼ of NE¼ NE¼ of NW¼	160	300
1880	29N	32E	25	N½ of SE¼ NE¼ of SW¼ SE¼ of NW¼	160	400
18811	24N	33E	4 5	NW¼ of SE¼ N½ of SW¼ NE¼ of SE¼	160	300
1881	30N	25E	34	Part	160	1,800

Year	Township	Range	Section	Parts of Sections	No. of Acres	Sale Price
1881	31N	36E	8	N½ of NW¼ SE¼ of NW¼ SW¼ of NE¼	160	480
1881	32N	35E	35 36	SE¼ of NE¼ S½ of NW¼ SW¼ of SE¼ N½ of SW¼ SE¼ of SW¼	640	95,500
			1	N½ of NE¼ NE¼ of NW¼ NW¼ of NE¼		
			8	SW¼ of NE¼ N½ of NW¼ SE¼ of NW¼		
			19	SE¼ of SE¼		
1881	23N	31E	2 15	SE¼ of SW¼ NE¼ of NW¼	80	500
1881	26N	34E	13	N½ of SE¼ N½ of SW¼	160	300
1881	31N	27E	35	W½ of SW¼ S½ of NW¼	160	300
1881	27N	25E	1	NE¼	160	350
1881	32N	35E	35 36	Part Part	120	360
1881	31N	26E	10 3	Part Part	160	250
1881	22N	33E	2 3	Part Part	160	400
1881	21N 22N	30E 30E	5 32	Part Part	160	500
1881	22N	34E 33E	6 1	Part Part	160	400
1881	25N	31E	13	SW¼ of NE¼ SE¼ of NW¼ NE¼ of SW¼	2,000	18,000

198

Year	Township	Range	Section	Parts of Sections	No. of Acres	Sales Price
	26N	33E	35 34	SW¼ of SW¼ S½ of SE¼ NW¼ of SE¼		
	25N	38E	9 10	E½ of SE¼ W½ of SW¼ N½ of NE¼		
	26N	33E	30 29	SE¼ of NE¼ SW¼ of NW¼		
	25N	33E	1	N½ of NW¼ SE¼ of SE¼		
	26N	33E	36	SE¼ SW¼		
			34 33	SE¼ of NW¼ SE¼ of NE¼ SE¼ of SW¼		
	25N	33E	35 2	S½ of SE¼ NE¼ of NE¼		
		32E	1	NE¼ of NE¼ N½ of NW¼		
		34E	6 22	NW¼ of NE¼ S½ of SE¼ SW¼ of SW¼		
		32E	23 26	SW¼ NW¼ of NW¼ NW¼ of NE¼		
	24N	33E	4 5	N½ of SW¼ NE¼ of SE¼		199
	25N	32E	28	SW¼ of SE¼		
1881	31N	36E	12 13	SE¼ of SW¼ NE¼ of NW¼ N½ of NE¼	160	480
1881	26N	27E	7 18	W½ of SW¼ W½ of NW¼	160	400
1881	24N	32E	36	SW¼ of NE¼ N½ of SE¼	120	300
1881	24N	34E	10	N½ of NE¼ N½ of NW¼	160	300
1881	24N	34E	12 13	W½ of SE¼ SE¼ of SE¼ NE¼ of NE¼	160	400
1881	30N	27E	3	NW¼ of NE¼ NE¼ of NW¼	160	300
	31N	27E	34	S½ of SW¼		

Year	Township	Range	Section	Parts of Sections	No. of Acres	Sales Price
1881	24N	34E	5	SW¼ of NW¼	160	300
				N½ of SW¼		
			6	NE¼ of SE¼		
1881	23N	33E	15	N½ of SW¼	1,760	7,680
				SW¼ of NW¼		
			16	SE¼ of NE¼		
		34E	24	S½ of NE¼		
				E½ of SE¼		
		33E	16	SW¼ of NE¼		
				E½ of NW¼		
				NW¼ of NW¼		
			25	SW¼		
	22N	33E	1	W½ of SW¼		
				SE¼ of SW¼		
				SW¼ of SE¼		
		34E	5	NW¼ of NE¼		
				N½ of NW¼		
				SW¼ of NW¼		
			6	S½ of NE¼		
				N½ of SE¼		
		33E	4	NE¼ of NE¼		
			3	N½ of NW¼		
				NW¼ of NE¼		
		34E	6	N½ of SW¼		
		33E	1	E½ of SE¼		
			2	W½ of NW¼		
			3	E½ of NE¼		
			2	SE¼ of NW¼		
				S½ of NE¼		
				NE¼ of SE¼		
1881	23N	25E	16	W½ of SW¼	160	1,000
			17	S½ of SE¼		
1881	23N	31E	10	SE¼ of SW¼	80	150
			15	NE¼ of NW¼		
1881	31N	26E	18	Part	160	500
1881	31N	26E	7	Part	160	500
1881	26N	27E	7	NE¼ of NE¼	120	500
			6	SE¼ of SE¼		
			5	SW¼ of SW¼		
1881	24N	34E	10	N½ of NE¼	160	1,000
				N½ of NW¼		

200

Year	Township	Range	Section	Parts of Sections	No. of Acres	Sales Price
1881	27N	28E	18	SE¼ of SE¼	160	300
			19	NE¼ of NE¼		
			20	N½ of NW¼		
1881	25N	24E	34	S½ of NE¼	160	200
				NW¼ of SE¼		
				NE¼ of SW¼		
1881	28N	25E	4	NW¼ of SW¼	80	500
			5	NE¼ of SE¼		
1881	25N	32E	28	SW¼ of SE¼	1,680	41,434
			22	S½ of SE¼		
			23	SW¼ of SW¼		
			26	NW¼ of NW¼		
				SW¼ of NE¼		
				SE¼ of NW¼		
		31E	13	NE¼ of SW¼		
		33E	1	NE¼ of NE¼		
				N½ of NW¼		
		34E	6	NW¼ of NE¼		
				SE¼ of SW¼		
	26N	34E	35	S½ of SE¼		
	25N	33E	2	NE¼ of NE¼		
				NE¼ of SW¼		
			34	S½ of NW¼		
	26N	33E	33	SE¼ of NE¼		
	25N	33E	1	N½ of NW¼		
				SE¼ of SW¼		
	26N	33E	36	SW¼ of SE¼		
				N½ of NE¼		
			30	SW¼ of NE¼		
			29	SE¼ of NW¼		
			9	E½ of SE¼		
	25N	33E	10	W½ of SW¼		
			35	SW¼ of SW¼		
				S½ of SE¼		
	26N	33E	34	NW¼ of SE¼		
			4	N½ of SW¼		
	24N	33E	5	NE¼ of SE¼		
				S½ of NE¼		
	25N	31E	25	NW¼ of SE¼		
1881	23N	34E	9	S½ of NE¼	320	2,150
				SE¼ of NW¼		
				NE¼ of SW¼		
			10	W½ of NW¼		
			3	S½ of SW¼		
1881	23N	32E	5	N½ of NW¼	120	400
			6	NE¼ of NE¼		

201

Year	Township	Range	Section	Parts of Sections	No. of Acres	Sales Price
1881	31N	27E	34	SW¼ of NE¼ SE¼ of NW¼ NE½ of SW¼ NW¼ of SE¼	160	400
1881	23N	32E	13	SW¼ of NW¼ S½ of NE¼	1,160	500
			14	SE¼ of NW¼		
			11	E½ of SE¼ NW¼ of SW¼		
			12	SW¼ of NW¼		
	24N	33E	32	SE¼ of NW¼ SW¼ of NE¼ N½ of SE¼		
		23E	23	N¼ of NW¼ W½ of NW¼		
			29	NE¼ of NE¼		
	23N	23E	9	W½ of NE¼ SE¼ of NE¼		
			10	SW¼ of NW¼		
		32E	13	N½ of SE¼ NE¼ of SE¼ NE¼ of SW¼ SE¼ of NW¼		
			14	SW¼ of NW¼ SE¼ of NW¼		
			15	N½ of NE¼		
1881	23N	32E	5	N½ of NE¼ SE¼ of NE¼	120	500
1881	25N	34E	5 6	N½ of NW¼ E½ of NE¼	160	500
1881	25N	31E	17	N½ of NW¼ N½ of NE¼	160	400
1881	31N	26E	7	Part	160	500
1881	31N	26E	17	Part	160	500
1881	31N	26E	18	Part	160	500
1881	31N	25E	13	Part	160	500
1881	29N	34E	26	SE¼	160	500
1881	26N	35E	16	W½ of NE¼ W½ of SE¼	160	400

202

Year	Township	Range	Section	Parts of Sections	No. of Acres	Sales Price	
1882	23N	20E	7	Part	160	90	
1882	32N	33E	30	Part	160	600	
1882	23N	19E	12 13	Part Part	160	115	
1882	24N	34E	12 13	Part Part	160	500	
1882	28N	35E	33	Part	160	200	
1882	26N	27E	31	Part	160	400	
1882	23N	19E 20E	1 6	Part Part	160	150	
1882	23N	19E	1	Part	160	130	
1882	26N	27E	32	Part	160	500	
1882	28N	35E	6	Part	160	650	
1882	31N	36E	21	Part	160	550	
1882	26N	23E	36	Part	140	300	203
1882	31N	35E	1	Part	160	600	
1882	26N	23E 24E	25 30	Part Part	160	300	
1882	23N	24E	8 17	Part Part	160	1,500	
1882	31N	36E	31	Part	160	600	
1882	32N	32E	24 25	Part Part	160	700	
1882	31N	27E	14 23	SW¼ of SE¼ SE¼ of SW¼ N½ of NW¼	160	400	
1882	27N	32E	12	S½ of SW¼	80	600	
1882	29N	24E	21	S½ of NW¼	80	700	
1882	27N	33E 32E	6 12 1	SE¼ S½ of SE¼ N½ of NE¼	320	2,500	

Year	Township	Range	Section	Parts of Sections	No. of Acres	Sale Price
1882	27N	32E	12	S½ of SW¼	80	600
1882	28N	32E	15 14	NE¼ of SW¼ NW¼ of SE¼	80	600
1882	28N	32E	21	N½ of SE¼	80	600
1882	28N	32E	7	E½ of SW¼	80	600
1882	32N	33E	29	Part	160	600
1882	32N	32E	23 24	Part Part	160	550
1882	31N	36E	9 8	Part Part	160	600
1882	31N	31N	5	Part	160	600
1882	27N	32E	11 12	Part Part	160	1,000
1882	32N	33E	22 27	Part Part	160	650
1882	23N	30E	12	Part	160	500
1882	25N	26E	3 4	Part Part	160	500
1882	24N	35E	28	SE¼	160	400
1882	23N	19E	2 1	Part Part	160	115
1882	23N	20E 19E	6 7 1 12	Part Part Part Part	160	150
1882	24N	23E	25	Part	160	1,500
1882	24N	23E	20 21	Part Part	160	1,000
1882	28N	32E	29	Part	160	500
1882	23N	32E	4	Part	160	1,000
1882	23N	19E	11	Part	160	180
1882	23N	20E	6 7	Part Part	160	100

204

Year	Township	Range	Section	Parts of Sections	No. of Acres	Sales Price
1882	29N	36E	20 29 28 21	Part Part Part Part	160	£1,900
1882	28N	32E	29 28	Part Part	80	600
1882	30N	28E	10	Part	160	750
1882	23N	19E	1 12	Part Part	160	195
1882	23N	19E	2	Part	160	180
1882	23N	19E	11	Part	160	114
1882	23N	19E 20E	12 7	Part Part	160	95
1882	23N	19E	12 11 14 13	Part Part Part Part	160	110
1882	23N	29E	7 18	Part Part	160	135
1882	31N	28E	10	Part	160	900
1882	27N	34E	6	Part	160	1,000
1882	30N	30E	22 23	Part Part	120	1,000
1882	30N	32E 36E	30 3	Part Part	90	650
1882	23N	20E	6	Part	160	160
1882	37N	29E	27	Part	120	1,000
1882	31N	39E	3 22 23	SW¼ of NW¼ NE¼ of NW¼ N½ of NE¼ N½ of NW¼ N½ of NE¼ S½ of SE¼	2,280	3,000

205

Year	Township	Range	Section	Parts of Sections	No. of Acres	Sales Price
			14	SE¼ of SW¼		
				W½ of SW¼		
				S½ of NE¼		
				NE¼ of SW¼		
			13	SE¼ of NW¼		
	29N	27E	10	W½ of SW¼		
			9	SE¼ of SE¼		
			16	E½ of NE¼		
				W½ of NE¼		
			15	NW¼ of SE¼		
				NE¼		
	31N	31E		NE¼ of SW¼		
				S½ of SW¼		
			14	SE¼		
			15	SE¼ of SE¼		
			22	NE¼ of NE¼		
				NW¼ of SW¼		
				S½ of NW¼		
				S½ of NE¼		
			18	E½ of SE¼		
				S½ of NW¼		
				N½ of SW¼		
				W½ of NE¼		
			13	NE¼ of NE¼		
				S½ of SW¼		
			17	S½ of SE¼		
			20	NW¼ of NE¼		
1883	30N	32E	29	Part	160	400
1883	24N	32E	30	Part	160	550
1883	26N	26E	15	Part	160	450
1883	23N	23E	8	Part	160	500
			9	Part		
1883	29N	24E	25	Part	800	20,000
			26	Part		
			27	Part		
			28	Part		
1883	28N	32E	18	Part	150	600
			13	Part		
1883	29N	31E	36	Part	160	600
1883	30N	25E	34	Part	612	10,000
			33	Part		
1883	30N	31E	24	Part	160	400

206

Year	Township	Range	Section	Parts of Sections	No. of Acres	24 Sales Price
1883	27N	25E	26	Part	160	500
			27	Part		
1883	31N	29E	22	Part	320	2,000
1883	26N	24E	21	Part	160	450
1883	26N	25E	3	Part	160	400
	27N	25E	34	Part		
1883	23N	31E	12	Part	160	1,437
1883	24N	32E	30	Part	160	950
1883	25N	24E	34	Part	160	1,600
			35	Part		
			26	Part		
1883	31N	27E	24	Part	200	500
			25	Part		
		28E	19	Part		
1883	25N	35E	5	Part	160	300
1883	25N	35E	6	Part	160	300
1883	28N	25E	10	Part	160	250
1883	28N	26E	8	Part	160	250
1883	28N	32E	1	$S\frac{1}{2}$ of $NE\frac{1}{4}$	160	500
				$NW\frac{1}{4}$ of $NW\frac{1}{4}$		
				$NW\frac{1}{4}$ of $SE\frac{1}{4}$		
1883	28N	34E	3	$W\frac{1}{2}$ of $NE\frac{1}{4}$	320	825
				$E\frac{1}{2}$ of $NE\frac{1}{4}$		
				$W\frac{1}{2}$ of $NW\frac{1}{4}$		
				$E\frac{1}{2}$ of $NW\frac{1}{4}$		
1883	28N	35E	33	Part	160	1,000
			34	Part		
			2	Part		
			35	Part		
	29N	36E	34	Part		
1883	28N	35E	33	Part	160	400
			34	Part		

Year	Township	Range	Section	Parts of Sections	No. of Acres	Sales Price
1883	31N	25E	20	W½ of NE¼ E½ of NW¼	160	600
1883	26N	26E	8 17	Part Part	160	500
1883	23N	30E	12	Part	160	700
1883	23N	31E	18	Part	160	600
1883	23N	31E	4 9	Part Part	160	1,625
1883	30N	30E	23	SW¼ of NW¼ N½ of NW¼ NE¼ of NE¼	160	850
1883	30N	30E	21	SE¼	160	775
1883	30N	30E	22	W½ of NW¼ N½ of SW¼	160	850
1883	28N	32E	5 6	N½ of SW¼ N½ of SE¼	160	700
1883	24N	31E	17	Part	160	1,625
1883	24N	31E	19	Part	160	650
1883	25N	25E	5	Part	160	500
1883	27N	27E	20	Part	160	500
1883	27N	25E	20 21 29	Part Part Part	160	450
1883	26N	24E	23	Part	160	500
1883	27N	25E	32	Part	160	425
1883	26N	24E	13	Part	160	475
1883	26N	26E	9	Part	160	450
1883	29N	26E	22 27	Part Part	120	250

208

Year	Township	Range	Section	Parts of Sections	No. of Acres	Sales Price
1883	28N	36E	2	Part	160	400
			35	Part		
	29N	36E	34	Part		
1883	30N	32E	33	Part	120	1,200
	29N	32E	5	Part		
1883	24N	32E	19	Part	160	950
1883	24N	31E	18	Part	160	700
1883	23N	31E	9	Part	634	6,500
			18	Part		
		30E	12	Part		
	24N	31E	18	Part		
1883	23N	31E	5	Part	160	625
			8	Part		
1883	28N	32E	3	S½ of SE¼	160	675
			10	NE¼ of NE¼		
			11	NW¼ of NW¼		
1883	28N	32E	4	S½ of NE¼	160	625
				S½ of NW¼		
1883	28N	32E	4	SW¼ of SW¼	160	600
				S½ of SE¼		
			5	SE¼ of SW¼		
1883	27N	33E	1	SW¼ of SE¼	160	825
				S½ of SW¼		
			2	SE¼ of SE¼		
1884	31N	27E	22	Part	160	300
1884	31N	27E	21	Part	160	300
1884	30N.	27E	2	S½ of NE¼	160	1,000
			1	S½ of NE¼		
1884	29N	27E	14	Part	160	200
1884	23N	20E	7	SE¼ of SE¼	160	200
			8	NE¼ of NE¼		
			17	NW¼ of NW¼		
			8	SW¼ of SW¼		
1884	23N	20E	6	SE¼ of SE¼	120	150
			7	SW¼ of SE¼		
			8	NE¼ of NE¼		

209

210

Year	Township	Range	Section	Parts of Sections	No. of Acres	Sales Price
1884	31N	25E	5	SW¼ of NW¼	120	300
				NW¼ of SW¼		
			6	NE¼ of SE¼		
1884	31N	24E	I	NE¼ of SE¼	120	500
				SE¼ of NE¼		
		25E	6	SE¼ of NE¼		
1884	31 N	15E	6	E½ of NE¼	640	19,000
				SW¼ of NE¼		
				NW¼ of NE¼		
				SW¼ of SE¼		
				E½ of SW¼		
		25E	6	NW¼ of SW¼		
		24E	1	SE¼ of SE¼		
				N½ of NE¼		
			12	SW¼ of NW¼		
				NE¼ of SW¼		
				NW¼ of SE¼		
				SE¼ of NW¼		
		25E	5	SW¼ of NE¼		
1884	31N	25E	6	E½ of NE¼	600	1,884
				SW¼ of NE¼		
				NW¼ of SE¼		
				SW¼ of SE¼		
				E½ of SW¼		
				NW¼ of SW¼		
			1	SE¼ of SE¼		
		24E	12	W½ of NE¼		
				NE¼ of SW¼		
				NW¼ of SE¼		
				SE¼ of NW¼		
		35E	5	SW¼ of NE¼		
1884	24N	19E	32	N½ of SE¼	160	200
			36	W½ of SW¼		
1884	30N	28E	19	S½ of NE¼	160	500
				NW¼ of NE¼		
				NE¼ of NW¼		
1884	26N	24E	30	SW¼ of SE¼	160	250
				W½ of SW¼		
			29	SE¼ of SW¼		
1884	28N	24E	29	S½ of SE¼	160	700
			28	SW¼ of SW¼		
			33	NW¼ of NW¼		

Year	Township	Range	Section	Parts of Sections	No. of Acres	Sales Price
1885	23N	31E	15	SE¼ of NW¼ SW¼ of NE¼ NW¼ of SW¼ NE¼ of SW¼	160	1,000
1885	26N	27E	10 15 9	W½ of SE¼ W½ of NE¼ SW¼ of SE¼	200	500
1885	23N	19E	9 ·4	W½ of NE¼ W½ of SE¼	160	400
1885	23N	19E	9	N½ of SE¼ N½ of SW¼	160	400
1886	31N	24E	28 21 22 23 22	NE¼ of NE¼ S½ of SE¼ NE¼ of SE¼ E½ of SW¼ W½ of SE¼ SE¼ of NW¼ NW¼ of SW¼	400	300
1886	31N	29E	21 28 22 23	S½ of NE¼ NE¼ of SE¼ NE¼ of SE¼ NE¼ of NE¼ NW¼ of NE¼ E½ of SW¼ W½ of SW¼ SE¼ of NW¼ NW¼ of SW¼	560	3,200
1886	30N	27E	10	N½ of SE¼ N½ of SW¼	160	300

211

MORA COUNTY

Year	Township	Range	Section	Parts of Sections	No. of Acres	Sales Price
1880	22N	36E	9	Part	160	225
1880	23N	31E	30	Part	160	250
			31	Part		
1880	22N	31E	5	Part	160	250
1881	22N	32E	10	SE¼ of NW¼	160	200
				SW¼ of NE¼		
				NE¼ of SW¼		
				NW¼ of SE¼		
1881	21N	34E	20	Part	160	400
			29	Part		
			30	Part		
1881	22N	31E	3	Part	4,840	5,000
			5	Part		
			9	Part		
			16	Part		
			13	Part		
	21N	31E	Parts of 9, 10, 11, 12, 1, 2,			
	23N	31E	Parts of 30, and 31.			
	22N	35E	Parts of 29, and 30.			
1881	21N	34E	Parts of 9, 10, 11, 12, 1, and 2.			
	22N	35E	All of Section 5 and 6.			
1881	23N	24E	20	Part	160	500
1881	22N	33E	1	Part	160	400
1881	22N	23E	28	E½ of NW¼	120	300
				SW¼ of NE¼		
1881	23N	24E	28	S½ of SW¼	160	40
			33	N½ of NW¼		
1881	22N	33E	30	Part	160	1,500
			29	Part		
			32	Part		
1881	21N	30E	5	Part	160	400
1881	21N	35E	5	SW¼ of SW¼	160	700
			6	S½ of SE¼		
				SE¼ of SW¼		
1881	21N	25E	4	SW¼	160	400
1881	21N	34E	21	Part	160	400
1881	20N	30E	10?	SE¼	160	500
1881	19N	32E	11	E½ of SE½	160	400
			12	W½ of SW¼		
1881	20N	30E	14	Part	160	400
1881	19N	32E	31	NE¼	160	300
1881	20N	30E	14	Part	160	400
1881	19N	32E	30	E½ of SE¼	160	350
				SW¼ of SE¼		
			29	NW¼ of SW¼		
1881	23N	25E	19	Part	160	600
			30	Part		

212

Year	Township	Range	Section	Parts of Sections	No. of Acres	Sales Price
1881	23N	24E	35	Part	160	400
			34	Part		
1881	21N	30E	17	Part	160	400
			16	Part		
			9	Part		
1881	22N	33E	4	Part	160	400
			3	Part		
1881	21N	30E	16	Part	160	500
1881	21N	30N	9	Part	160	500
			8	Part		
1881	22N	34E	24	Part	160	350
1881	21N	30E	21	Part	160	400
			16	Part		
1881	21N	30E	31	Part	160	400
			30	Part		
1881	21S	29E	13	Part	160	500
			24	Part		
1881	22N	34E	16	Part	160	300
			15	Part		
1881	22N	33E	33	Part	160	350
			4	Part		
1881	22N	34E	2	Part	160	225
			3	Part		
1881	22N	34E	11	Part	160	250
			2	Part		
1881	21N	30E	32	Part	160	400
			31	Part		
1881	21N	29E	14	Part		
			13	Part		
1881	22N	32E	14	Part	160	400
1881	22N	30E	22	Part	160	400
			23	Part		
1881	21N	34E	9	Part	160	500
			8	Part		
1881	21N	34E	15	Part	160	500
			10	Part		
1881	22N	30E	27	Part	160	400
1881	21N	34E	10	Part	160	500
			9	Bart		
1881	22N	33E	29	Part	160	400
			32	Part		
1881	21N	30E	21	Part	160	500
1881	23N	34E	33	Part	160	300
			32	Part		
1881	23N	34E	33	Part	160	300
1881	21N	30E	28	Part	160	400
1881	21N	29E	36	Part	160	400
			25	Part		
1881	22N	34E	3	Part	160	325

213

Year	Township	Range	Section	Parts of Sections	No. of Acres	Sales Price
1881	23S	34E	33	SE¼ of SW¼	800	600
			32	E½ of SE¼		
				SW¼ of SE¼		
			33	NE¼ of SW¼		
				W½ of SE¼		
				SE¼ of SE¼		
	22S	34E	33	W½ of SE¼		
				E½ of NW¼		
			2	S½ of SW¼		
			3	E½ of NE¼		
			11	SW¼ of SE¼		
			2	SW¼ of SE¼		
				E½ of SE¼		
1882	20N	31E	30	N½ of NE¼	160	70
				SW¼ of NE¼		
				NE¼ of SW¼		
1882	23N	25	19	Part	160	500
1882	21N	36E	32	Part	80	600
1882	22N	24E	36	S½ of SE¼	160	500
				S½ of SW¼		
1882	20N	30E	14	Part	480	500
			24	Part		
			13	Part		
			10	Part		
1882	20N	35E	6	N½ of SW¼	160	500
			1	E½ of SE¼		
1882	21N	34E	11	SW¼ of NE¼	160	600
				S½ of NW¼		
				NW¼ of SW¼		
1882	19N	29E	2	Part	160	395
1882	19N	35E	22	N½ of NW¼	640	4,188
				N½ of NE¼		
			16	SW¼ of SW¼		
			20	NE¼ of NE¼		
			21	N½ of NW¼		
			14	SW¼ of SE¼		
				S½ of SW¼		
				NE¼ of SW¼		
			8	SE¼ of NW¼		
			17	N½ of NW¼		
				NW¼ of NE¼		
1882	19N	35E	16	SW¼ of SW¼	160	500
			20	NE¼ of NE¼		
			21	N½ of NW¼		
1882	18N	29E	20	W½ of NW¼	160	250
				SE¼ of NW¼		
				NE¼ of SW¼		
1882	18N	29E	17	W½ of SW¼	160	350
				SE¼ of SW¼		
				SW¼ of SE¼		

214

Year	Township	Range	Section	Parts of Sections	No. of Acres	Sales Price
1882	18N	29E	30	E½ of NW¼ SE¼ of NE¼ NW¼ of SE¼	160	300
1882	19N	35E	22	N½ of NW¼ N½ of NE¼	640	2,900
			16	SW¼ of SW¼		
			20	NE¼ of NE¼		
			21	N½ of NW¼		
			8	SE¼ of SW¼		
			14	S½ of SW¼ NE¼ of SW¼ SW¼ of SE¼		
			17	N½ of NW¼ NW¼ of NE¼		
1882	18N	29E	27	NE¼ of SW¼	160	300
			22	SE¼ of SW¼ W½ of SE¼		
1882	18N	29E	18	SW¼ of SW¼	160	350
			19	W½ of NW¼ NW¼ of SW¼		
1882	23N	24E	25	E½ of NE¼ SE¼ of NE¼ NW¼ of SE¼	160	1,055
1882	23N	25E	17	SW¼ of SW¼	160	1,055
			20	N½ of NW¼ SW¼ of NW¼		
1882	22N	33E	21	Part	160	250
1882	22N	33E	18	Part	160	220
			19	Part		
1882	22N	30E	7	Part	160	650
			18	Part		
1882	22N	30E	5	Part	160	700
			6	Part		
			7	Part		
1882	22N	30E	30	Part	160	650
1882	20N	30E	14	Part	160	400
1882	21N	34E	2	Part	160	800
			11	Part		
1882	21N	34E	12	Part	160	900
1882	20N	30E	24	Part	160	500
1882	18N	30E	10	Part	160	500
1882	18N	26E	17	Part	160	1,000
			8	Part		
1882	18N	26E	17	Part	160	1,000
1882	20N	20E	33	Part	160	400
1882	20N	29E	34	Part	160	400
1882	18N	26E	21	Part	160	1,000
1882	18N	26E	36	Part	160	1,000
1882	18N	30E	10	Part	160	500
1882	21N	34E	6	Part	160	800
1882	19N	34E	12	Part	160	800

Year	Township	Range	Section	Parts of Sections	No. of Acres	Sales Price
1882	23N	32E	36	Part	160	600
1882	18N	29E	22	N½ of NE¼	160	175
				SE¼ of NE¼		
			3	NW¼ of NW¼		
1883	22N	24E	22	SE¼ of NE¼	160	525
				NE¼ of SE¼		
			23	S½ of NE¼		
1883	23N	23E	27	SE¼ of NW¼	320	1,000
				E½ of SW¼		
			34	NE¼ of NW¼		
			27	S½ of NE¼		
				NE¼ of NE¼		
			26	NW¼ of NW¼		
1883	22N	33E	21	Part	160	250
1883	21N	34E	10	S½ of NE¼	160	600
				S½ of NW¼		
1883	23N	19E	29	NW¼	160	300
1883	19N	26E	26	NE¼	320	2,000
			23	E½ of SE¼		
				S½ of NE¼		
1883	22N	25E	5	N½ of NE¼	166	175
				N½ of NW¼		
1883	23N	25E	31	E½ of SE¼	160	1,000
				NW¼ of SE¼		
				SW¼ of NE¼		
1883	22N	25E	4	SW¼ of NE¼	160	1,150
				S½ of NW¼		
				NW¼ of NW¼		
1883	23N	24E	25	SE¼ of NW¼	160	1,100
				E½ of SW¼		
			38	NE¼ of NW¼		
1883	23N	23E	27	S½ of NE¼	160	500
				NE¼ of NE¼		
			26	NW¼		
1883	22N	24E	35	W½ of NE¼	160	500
				W½ of SW¼		
1883	22N	23E	12	S½ of NE¼	160	500
				NE¼ of NE¼		
			1	SE¼ of SE¼		
1883	22N	23E	11	NE¼ of SW¼	160	500
				W½ of SE¼		
				SE¼ of SE¼		
1883	22N	25E	3	N½ of SW¼	160	1,500
			4	W½ of SE¼		
1883	22N	23E	13	E½ of SW¼	160	500
				SE¼ of NW¼		
				SW¼ of NE¼		
1883	22N	19E	9	NE¼ of NE¼	160	2,000
			10	NW¼ of NW¼		
			4	E½ of SE¼		
1883	19N	35E	8	Part	160	500
			17	Part		

216

Year	Township	Range	Section	Parts of Sections	No. of Acres	Sales Price
1883	22N	32E	32	N½ of SE¼	160	200
				SE¼ of SE¼		
			15	N½ of NE¼		
1883	22N	31E	3	W½ of SW¼	5,000	5,000
				S½ of NW¼		
			5	N½ of SW¼		
				SE¼ of SW¼		
				SW¼ of SE¼		
			9	W½ of NW¼		
				N½ of SW¼		
				SE¼ of SW¼		
				SW¼ of SE¼		
			16	N½ of NE¼		
			13	SW¼ of SW¼		
			30	SE¼ of SW¼		
	23N	31E	31	E½ of NW¼		
				NE¼ of SW¼		
				S½ of NW¼		
				S½ of NE¼		
				N½ of SE¼		
			15	NE¼ of SW¼		
			9	N½ of SE¼		
				S½ of NW¼		
				S½ of NE¼		
				N½ of SE¼		
			10	SW¼		
				S½ of NW¼		
				S½ of NE¼		
				NE¼		
				N½ of SW¼		
				SE¼ of SW¼		
			11	N½ of SE¼		
			12	N½ of N½ of NW¼		
				N½ of NE¼		
			1	S½ of SW¼		
				S½ of SE¼		
	21N	34E	2	SE¼ of SE¼		
		35E	5	All of		
			6	All of		
	22N	35E	29	All of		
			32	All of		
1884	20N	25E	26	N½ of NW¼	160	1,700
				N½ of NE¼		
1884	22N	19E	5	Part	279	4,000
			8	Part		
1884	20N	31E	11	S½ of NE¼	160	750
				N½ of SE¼		
1884	20N	31E	11	SW¼ of SE¼	160	250
				S½ of SW¼		
			14	NW¼ of NW¼		
1884	23N	32E	30	NE¼	160	300

217

Year	Township	Range	Section	Parts of Sections	No. of Acres	Sale Price
1884	20N	31E	12	NW¼ of NE¼ NE¼ of NW¼ S½ of NW¼	160	75
1884	22N	33E	35	S½ of SW¼ S½ of SE¼	160	75
1884	22N	19E	4	NW¼ of SE¼ SW¼ of NE¼ S½ of NW¼	160	10
1884	19N	22E	15	W½ of NE¼ SW¼ of NE¼	160	1
1884	21N	33E	28	N½ of SW¼ SE¼ of SW¼ NE¼ of SW¼	160	1,80
1884	23N	19E	33 32	E½ of SE¼ NW¼ of SE¼ NE¼ of SW¼	160	10
1884	22N	33E	36	W½ of SW¼ W½ of NW¼	160	1,00
1884	21N	33E	2 1	E½ of NE¼ S½ of NW¼	160	1,00
1884	20N	31E	11	S½ of NE¼ N½ of SE¼	160	75
1884	20N	31E	11	SW¼ of SE¼ S½ of SW¼	160	25
			14	NW¼ of NW¼		
1884	18N	20E	6	SW¼	160	1,50
1884	23N	31E	15	SE¼ of SW¼ SW¼ of NE¼ NW¼ of SE¼ NE¼ of SW¼	480	5,00
			14	S½ of NE¼ N½ of SE¼		
			21	N½ of NE¼ SW¼ of NE¼ SE¼ of NW¼		
			22	N½ of SE¼ SE¼ of SE¼		
			27	NE¼ of NE¼		
1884	23N	19E	29	NW¼	160	40
1884	18N	20E	5	½ of SW¼	80	60
1884	23N	18E	8 7	Part Part	320	1,00
1885	22N	33E	34	N½ of NW¼ N½ of NE¼	160	50
1885	19N	31E	5	W½ of NW¼ W½ of SW¼	160	23
1885	21N	30E	30	Part	160	20
1885	22N	31E	25	W½ of NW¼ SE¼ of NW¼ SW¼ of NE¼	160	40

218

Year	Township	Range	Section	Parts of Sections	No. of Acres	Sales Price
1885	21N	31E	26	S½ of SW¼	160	750
			35	N½ of NW¼		
1885	22N	32E	32	E½ of NW¼	160	1,000
				S½ of NE¼		
1885	19N	23E	29	SE¼ of SW¼	160	1,000
				N½ of SW¼		
			30	NE¼ of SE¼		
1885	22N	31E	33	SE¼ of NW¼	160	200
				SW¼ of NE¼		
				W½ of SE¼		
1885	22N	31E	36	S½ of SW¼	160	200
				S½ of SE¼		
1885	19N	29E	28	Part	160	200
1885	19N	29E	28	Part	160	200
1885	21N	34E	20	NW¼	160	875
1885	23N	30E	23	SE¼ of NE¼	160	1,000
				E½ of SE¼		
			26	NE¼ of NE¼		
1885	18N	20E	5	S½ of SE¼	80	500
1885	22N	33E	28	Part	320	2,000
			33	Part		
1885	22N	33E	28	Part	160	800
1885	22N	33E	34	Part	160	2,000
1885	22N	33E	33	Part	160	1,000
1885	23N	19E	9	W½ of NE¼	160	400
			4	W½ of SE¼		
1886	19N	29E	22	SW¼ of SW¼	160	200
				S½ of SW¼		
				NW¼ of SW¼		
1886	21N	35E	10	Part	160	500
			9	Part		
1886	20N	31E	30	Part	160	635
			29	Part		
1886	22N	19E	4	Part	160	325
	23N	19E	33	Part		
1886	21N	45E	8	Part	160	500
			5	Part		
1886	21N	24E	29	Part	160	500
1887	21N	35E	5	Part	160	800
			6	Part		
1887	23N	18E	33	SE¼	160	1,000
1887	21N	34E	19	Part	162	500
		33E	24	Part		
1887	22N	32E	32	N½ of SE¼	160	100
				SE¼ of SE¼		
			15	NE¼ of NE¼		
1887	22N	32E	10	SE¼ of NW¼	160	200
				SW¼ of NE¼		
				NE¼ of SW¼		
				NW¼ of SE¼		

219

Year	Township	Range	Section	Parts of Sections	No. of Acres	Sales Price
1887	22N	32E	10	Part	160	100
			15	Part		
1887	23N	31E	14	$S\frac{1}{2}$ of $NE\frac{1}{4}$	800	7,200
				$N\frac{1}{2}$ of $SE\frac{1}{4}$		
			21	$N\frac{1}{2}$ of $NE\frac{1}{4}$		
				$SW\frac{1}{4}$ of $NE\frac{1}{4}$		
			22	$N\frac{1}{2}$ of $SE\frac{1}{4}$		
				$SE\frac{1}{4}$ of $SE\frac{1}{4}$		
			27	$NE\frac{1}{4}$ of $NW\frac{1}{4}$		
				$N\frac{1}{2}$ of $SE\frac{1}{4}$		
				$S\frac{1}{2}$ of $NE\frac{1}{4}$		
			19	$SE\frac{1}{4}$ of $SE\frac{1}{4}$		
			34	$N\frac{1}{2}$ of $SE\frac{1}{4}$		
				$SW\frac{1}{4}$ of $NE\frac{1}{4}$		
				$SE\frac{1}{4}$ of $SW\frac{1}{4}$		
1887	20N	22E	8	$N\frac{1}{2}$	120	5,000
				$N\frac{1}{2}$ of $SE\frac{1}{4}$		
				$N\frac{1}{2}$ of $SW\frac{1}{4}$		

220

SAN MIGUEL COUNTY

Year	Township	Range	Section	Parts of Sections	No. of Acres	Sales Price
1878	8N	21E	11	N½ of SW¼	80	50
1881	13N	36E	10	S½ of SW¼	80	600
1882	18N	30E	15	Part	160	500
1882	4N	20E	5	S½ of SW¼	160	600
			6	S½ of SE¼		
1882	13N	34E	2	N½ of SE¼	80	600
1882	18N	30E	4	Part	160	500
			9	Part		
1882	19N	30E	29	Part	160	500
1882	19N	30E	18	Part	160	500
			19	Part		
1882	15N	31E	8	Part	160	650
1882	17N	30E	36	Part	160	800
1882	16N	30E	12	Part	160	700
1882	15N	31E	10	Part	160	800
1882	13N	34E	5	Part	160	800
1882	16N	30E	2	Part	143	800

221

Year	Township	Range	Section	Parts of Sections	No. of Acres	Sales Price
1882	17N	29E	24	Part	160	800
1882	13N	36E	10	N½ of SE¼	80	600
1882	17N	30E	30	Part	120	750
1882	17N	30E	20	Part	120	750
1882	13N	36E	8	N½ of NE¼	80	600
1882	17N	30E	24	Part	120	750
1882	13N	36E	8	N½ of NW¼	80	600
1882	13N	36E	14 / 10	NE¼ of NW¼ SW¼ of SE¼	80	600
1882	13N	35E	2	Part	120	900
1882	13N	36E	6	N½ of SE¼	80	600
1882	7N	23E	22	NE¼ of NW¼ W½ of NE¼ NW¼ of SE¼	160	200
1882	7N	23E	10	Part	160	200
1882	9N	22E	32 / 31	NW¼ of SW¼ E½ of SW¼	160	200
1882	13N	36E	14	N½ of NE¼	80	600
1882	13N	34E	6	Part	160	867
1882	13N	36E	12	W½ of NW¼	80	600
1882	13N	36E	6	NE¼ of NW¼ SW¼ of NE¼	80	600
1882	10N	35E	24	Part	160	500
1882	13N	36E	11	Part	160	800
1882	13N	35E	6	NE¼ of SE¼ NW¼ of SE¼	118	897

222

Year	Township	Range	Section	Parts of Sections	No. of Acres	Sales Price
1882	10N	26E	12	N½ of SW¼ E½ of NW¼	160	500
1882	18N	30E	22	E½ of NE¼ E½ of SE¼	160	500
1882	18N	26E	36 25	NW¼ of NW¼ SW¼ of NW¼ W½ of SW¼	160	1,000
1882	13N	34E	12	N½ of NE¼	80	600
1882	14N	30E	24	E½ of NW¼	80	300
1882	17N	30E	12	SW¼	160	100
1882	18N	30E	27	E½ of NE¼ E½ of SE¼	160	500
1882	13N	34E	1	SE¼	160	1,000
1882	13N	36E	9 16	Part Part	170	1,000
1882	18N	26E	36	Part	160	1,000
1882	17N	29E	8	Part	160	1,500
1882	13N	35E	3	Part	160	1,000
1882	17N	31E	17	Part	160	550
1882	18N	21E	23	Part	160	1,000
1882	13N	35E	5	Part	160	1,000
1882	17N	31E	19	Part	160	580
1882	13N	35E	1	NE¼	160	1,000
1882	13N	35E	7	NW¼	160	1,000

223

Year	Township	Range	Section	Parts of Sections	No. of Acres	Sales Price
1882	13N	34E	3	Part	160	1,000
1882	12N	24E	29 32	Part Part	320	200
1882	13N	34E	7	Part	160	1,000
1882	15N	31E	13	Part	160	1,000
1882	13N	34E	11	Part	160	1,000
1882	17N	31E	30 19	W$\frac{1}{2}$ of NW$\frac{1}{4}$ NE$\frac{1}{4}$ of NW$\frac{1}{4}$ SE$\frac{1}{4}$ SW$\frac{1}{4}$ of SW$\frac{1}{4}$	160	595
1882	17N	31N	29 30	W$\frac{1}{2}$ of NW$\frac{1}{4}$ NW$\frac{1}{4}$ of SW$\frac{1}{4}$ NE$\frac{1}{4}$ of NE$\frac{1}{4}$	160	450
1882	17N	31E	8 17	SW$\frac{1}{4}$ of SE$\frac{1}{4}$ NE$\frac{1}{4}$	160	600
1882	13N	24E	24	S$\frac{1}{2}$ of S$\frac{1}{2}$	160	500
1882	18N	30E	26 35	SW$\frac{1}{4}$ pf SW$\frac{1}{4}$ N$\frac{1}{2}$ of NW$\frac{1}{4}$ SW$\frac{1}{4}$ of NW$\frac{1}{4}$	160	500
1882	10N	26E	2	SE$\frac{1}{4}$	160	500
1882	11N	33E	16	NW$\frac{1}{4}$	160	100
1882	11N	33E	16	SE$\frac{1}{4}$	160	100
1882	11N	33E	10	SE$\frac{1}{4}$	160	100
1882	11N	33E	16	NE$\frac{1}{4}$	160	100
1882	12N	24E	4	SE$\frac{1}{4}$	160	50
1882	17, 18N	30E	2 34 12	NE$\frac{1}{4}$ N$\frac{1}{2}$ of NE$\frac{1}{4}$ N$\frac{1}{2}$ of NW$\frac{1}{4}$ SW$\frac{1}{4}$	479	3,000
1882	17N	30E	11	E$\frac{1}{2}$ of NE$\frac{1}{4}$ W$\frac{1}{2}$ of NW$\frac{1}{4}$	160	1,000

224

Year	Township	Range	Section	Parts of Sections	No. of Acres	Sales Price
1882	18N	30E	34	N½ of NE¼ N½ of NW¼	160	100
1882	17N	30E	4 1	E½ of SE¼ S½ of SW¼	160	100
1882	18N	30E	28	N½ of SE¼ N½ of SW¼	160	100
1882	17N	31E	8 5	NW¼ of NE¼ W½ of SE¼	120	595
1882	17N	31E	8	S½ of NW¼ SW¼ of NE¼ NE¼ of SW¼	160	390
1882	17N	31E	5	W½ of NE¼ E½ of NW¼	160	475
1882	13N	36E	1	Part	160	850
1882	16N	39E	26	Part	160	700
1882	16N	30E	36	Part	160	700
1883	10N	36E	22	SE¼	160	100
1883	10N	36E	16	Part	160	100
1883	15N	22E	30	Part	160	100
1883	14N	22E	9	Part	160	100
1883	11N	33,32E	16 18 20 24	Part Part Part Part	960	3,900
1883	15N	22E	32	Part	160	100
1883	11N	36E	34	W½ of NE¼ NE¼ of SE¼ SE¼ of NE¼	160	100
1883	12N	33E	28	E½ of SW¼ W½ of SE¼	160	650

225

Year	Township	Range	Section	Parts of Sections	No. of Acres	Sales Price
1883	12N	30E	25	S½ of SE¼ S½ of SW¼	320	1,000
			35	N½ of NE¼ N½ of NW¼		
1883	12N	33E	36	Part	160	425
1883	11N	32E	22	Part	160	425
1883	11N	33E	19	SW¼	160	400
1883	11N	33E	22	Part	160	450
1883	10N	35E	1	Part	159	100
1883	11N	33E	9 10 16	Part Part Part	960	3,900
1883	1CN	36E	8	Part	160	100
1883	11N	33E	16	NW¼	160	100
1883	11N	33E	20	NE¼	160	100
1883	11N	32E	24	SW¼ NW¼ SE¼ NE¼	2880	12,000
		33E	4	SE¼ SE¼		
			9	NE¼ NW¼ SW¼		
			10	NE¼		
			16	NW¼ SE¼ SW¼ NE¼		
			20	NW¼ SE¼		
			18	NE¼		
			24	E½ of SW¼		
	12N	33E	28	W½ of SE¼		
1883	12N	33E	2	SW¼	160	200
1883	11N	33E	3	W½ of SW¼ W½ of NW¼	160	200

226

Year	Township	Range	Section	Parts of Sections	No. of Acres	Sales Price	
1883	11N	33E	25	N½ of SE¼ E½ of NE¼	160	200	
1883	10N	32E	9 3	NE¼ of NE¼ SE¼ of SE¼ S½ of SW¼	160	200	
1883	11N	33E	12	S½ of NW¼ N½ of SW¼	160	200	
1883	10N	33E	21	Part	160	200	
1883	11N	33E	18	SE¼	160	100	
1883	11N	36E	31	Part	160	100	
1883	11N	33E	16	SW¼	160	100	
1883	11N	33E	20	NW¼	160	100	
1883	10N	36E	20	Part	160	100	
1883	10N	36E	18	SE¼	160	100	
1883	11N	33E	19 24	NW¼ of SW¼ N½ of SW¼ N½ of SE¼ NE¼ of SW¼	240	225	227
1883	13N	24E	24	S½ of SE¼ S½ of SW¼	160	200	
1883	11N	33E	35	N½ of NW¼	80	225	
1883	11N	32E	24	NE¼	160	100	
1883	11N	36E	32	Part	160	400	
1883	13N	22E	14	Part	160	820	
1883	13N	36E	5	Part	160	500	
1883	13N	36E	7	NE¼	160	500	
1883	10N	36E	6	Part	160	100	
1883	11N	32E	24	SE¼	160	100	

Year	Township	Range	Section	Parts of Sections	No. of Acres	Sales Price
1883	11N	32E	24	NW¼	160	100
1883	13N	36E	2 11	Part Part	160	500
1883	13N	34E	7	Part	160	500
1883	13N	34E	5	Part	160	500
1883	13N	34E	11	Part	160	500
1883	13N	36E	15	Part	160	500
1883	13N	34E	1	Part	160	500
1883	11N	30E	3	Part	160	200
1883	14N	22E	4	Part	160	100
1883	11N	30E	8	Part	160	200
1884	11N	29E	13	Part	160	2,650
1884	13N	22E	14	Part	120	400
1884	12N 11N	33E 32E	22 2	Part Part	120	1,200
1884	14N	22E	6	Part	80	250
1884	17N	31E	20	S½ of SE¼ S½ of SW¼	160	10,000
1884	11,12N	32,33,34E	31 32 29 28 22 19 27 36 33 27	Part Part Part Part Part Part Part Part Part Part	1,279	5,000
1884	15N	22E	30	Part	80	300
1884	14N	35E	36	Part	160	4,000
1884	13N	36E	4	Part	160	700

228

Year	Township	Range	Section	Parts of Sections	No. of Acres	Sales Price
1884	11N	33	29	Part	2560	4,500
			17	Part		
			27	Part		
			26	Part		
			16	Part		
		31E	25	Part		
	10N	33E	21	Part		
		32E	6	Part		
		31E	1	Part		
	12N	33E	2	Part		
			28	Part		
			32	Part		
		34E	27	Part		
1884	12N	33E	33	Part	160	375
1884	13N	22E	3	Part	160	700
1884	12N	24E	6	Part	119	400
		23E	10	Part		
	13N	22E	14	Part		
1885	9N	23E	32	NW$\frac{1}{4}$ of SW$\frac{1}{4}$	160	500
			31	E$\frac{1}{2}$ of SE$\frac{1}{4}$		
				SW$\frac{1}{4}$ of SE$\frac{1}{4}$		
1885	13N	25E	6	Part	80	500
1885	19N	35E	14	NE$\frac{1}{4}$ of SE$\frac{1}{4}$	80	800
	18N	31E	28	NE$\frac{1}{4}$ of NW$\frac{1}{4}$		
1885	17N	31E	30	Part	320	10,000
			20	Part		
1885	13N	25E	32	Part	160	400
1885	15N	22E	3	SW$\frac{1}{4}$	160	800
1885	13N	23E	3	Part	160	500
1885	13N	25E	6	Part	80	300
1885	14N	22E	16	E$\frac{1}{2}$ of NE$\frac{1}{4}$	120	900
				NE$\frac{1}{4}$ of SE$\frac{1}{4}$		
1885	13N	24E	24	S$\frac{1}{2}$ of S$\frac{1}{2}$	160	1,000
1885	16	11	28	Part	160	4,022
1885	11N	29E	13	N$\frac{1}{2}$ of NE$\frac{1}{2}$	160	1,500
				NW of NW		

229

Year	Township	Range	Section	Parts of Sections	No. of Acres	Sales Price
1885	12N	30E	25	S½ of SE¼ S½ of SW¼ N½ of NW¼	240	2,000
1885	12N	30E	26	Part	160	1,000
1885	10N	25E	26	Part	120	625
1885	14N 13N	24E 24E	34 3	Part Part	162	200
1885	7N	25E	30	Part	80	1,400
1885	13N	24E	24	Part	160	1,000
1886	12N	30E	35	N½ of NE¼	80	500
1886	12N	30E	34	SE¼	160	500
1886	13N	24E	24	S½ of S½	160	666
1886	10N	35E	24 32	Part Part	320	3,000
1886	13N	22E 23E	3 7	Part Part	160	400

230

LAS ANIMAS COUNTY

Year	Township	Range	Section	Parts of Sections	No. of Acres	Sales Price	
1870	32S	61W	7	SW¼	160	1,500	
1873	33S	63W	35	SE¼	160	800	
1873	33S	63W	35	NW¼	160	700	
1873	33S	63W	35	NE¼	160	600	
1873	33S	63W	35	SW¼	160	600	
1873	32S	63W	28	S½ of NE¼	80	560	
1873	32S	64W	34	S½ of NE¼	160	900	
				N½ of SE¼			
1873	32S	63W	29	N½ of SE¼	160	900	
				SW¼ of SE¼			
				SE¼ of SW¼			
1873	33S	63W	29	¼ of SE	160	1,000	
1873	33S	63W	28	SE¼	160	800	
1873	32S	63W	21	SE¼ of SW¼	160	1,000	
			28	E½ of NW¼			
				E¼ of SW¼			
1873	32S	63W	20	SE¼ of SE¼	160	800	
			21	N½ of SW¼			
				SW¼ of SW¼			
1873	33S	64W	11	W½ of NW¼	160	900	
				N½ of SW¼			
1873	33S	64W	2	SW¼ of NE¼	160	800	231
				SE¼ of NW¼			
				W½ of SE¼			
1873	32S	63W	28	W½ of NW¼	160	800	
			29	E½ of NE¼			
1873	32S	63W	28	NW¼ of SW¼	160	900	
				S½ of SW¼			
			29	SE¼ of SE¼			
1873	32S	63W	32	NW¼	160	800	
1873	32S	64W	7	S½ of NE¼	160	800	
				N½ of SE¼			
1873	32S	64W	7	SW¼	151	800	
1873	32S	64W	34	SW¼	160	600	
1873	33S	64W	3	Part	159	960	
1873	33S	64W	3	Part	160	800	
1873	33S	64W	9	SW¼ of NE¼	160	800	
				N½ of SE¼			
				SE¼ of SE¼			
1873	33S	64W	9	N½ of NE¼	160	800	
				SE¼ of NE¼			
			10	NW¼ of NW¼			
1873	32S	63W	21	Part	160	640	
1873	33S	64W	2	Part	120	800	
1873	32S	64W	34	Part	160	1,000	
			35	Part			
1873	33S	64W	10	Part	120	950	
1873	32S	65W	1	Part	159	800	
1873	33S	63W	6	N½ of NE¼	153	1,000	
				E¼ of NW¼			

Year	Township	Range	Section	Parts of Sections	No. of Acres	Sales Price
1873	34S	64W	7	SW¼ of NW¼ W½ of SW¼ SE¼ of SW¼	120	650
1873	32S	63W	28	N½ of NE¼	80	480
1873	34S	64W	1	E½ of SW¼ W½ of SE¼	160	800
1873	33S	63W	25	NW¼	160	450
1873	32S	63W	33	W½ of SW¼	80	560
1873	33S	63W	34	SW¼	160	400
1873	33S	63W	34	NW¼	160	500
1873	32S	65W	1 2	S½ of NW¼ NE¼ of SW¼ SE¼ of NE¼	160	800
1874	33S	63W	34	E½ of NE¼ E½ of SE¼	160	400
1874	33S	63W	26	Part	160	425
1874	33S	63W	27	NE¼	160	424
1874	33S	63W	27	Part	160	450
1874	33S	63W	26	Part	160	375
1874	33S	63W	26	Part	160	400
1874	33S	63W	34	Part	160	500
1874	33S	63W	26	Part	160	500
1874	34S	64W	2	Part	160	600
1874	33S	64W	18	SW¼ of NE¼ NE¼	120	500
1874	32S	64W	11	SE¼ of SW¼ NE½ of SE¼	120	1,200
1874	32S	64W	34 35	N½ of NE¼ W½ of NW¼	160	400
1874	34S	63W	11	SW¼	160	715
1874	32S	63W	20 29	S½ of SW¼ SW¼ of SE¼ NW¼ of NW¼	160	1,200
1874	33S	63W	30	2/3 of S½ of NE¼	80	800
1874	34S	63W	11	SE¼	160	630
1874	34S	63W	11	NW¼	160	800
1874	32S	64W	34	Part	160	1,000
1874	32S	64W	27	W½ of SW¼ SE¼ of SW¼ SW¼ of SE¼	160	1,000
1874	33S	63W	29	E½ of NE¼	80	800
1874	33S	63W	29	NW¼	160	1,500
1874	32S	64W	26 27	S½ of SW¼ E½ of SE¼	160	1,000
1874	33S	64W	29	SW¼	160	1,100
1874	32S	63W	32	SW¼	160	1,100
1874	34S	63W	11	NE¼	160	600
1874	34S	63W	11	SE¼	160	630
1874	34S	64W	7	SW¼ of NW¼ W½ of SW¼ SE¼ of SW¼	160	600

232

Year	Township	Range	Section	Parts of Sections	No. of Acres	Sales Price
1874	33S	63W	36	SW¼	160	325
1874	23S	63W	36	NW¼	160	350
1874	33S	63W	25	SW¼	160	535
1874	32S	63W	See last page Las Animas County			
1875	32S	63W	31	E½ of SW¼	240	600
				E½ of NW¼		
				E½ of SW¼		
1875	33S	63W	5	NE¼	160	400
1875	33S	63W	34	SE¼	160	370
1875	34S	62W	19	SE¼	160	300
1875	32S	64W	22	SE¼ of SE¼	160	1,350
			23	SW¼ of SW¼		
			26	N½ of NW¼		
1875	31S	59W	33	S½ of SE¼	160	350
			34	NE¼ of SE¼		
				NW¼ of SW¼		
1875	32S	61W	34	E½ of NE¼	160	350
				NW¼ of NE¼		
			35	NW¼ of NW¼		
1875	32S	63W	31	NE¼	160	800
1875	34S	64W	2	NW¼	160	1,108
1875	33S	64W	2	N½ of NE¼	160	450
			3	S½ of SE¼		
1875	34S	63W	2	SW¼	160	400
1875	34S	62W	7	SW¼	160	300
1875	34S	62W	20	SW¼	160	300
1875	33S	63W	30	S½ of SW¼	160	800
1875	34S	62W	18	N½ of SE¼	160	150
1875	33S	64W	9	E½ of SE¼	.80	420
1875	30S	65W	27	W½ of SE¼	160	1,200
1875	32S	63W	30	E½ of NW¼	160	600
				E½ of SW¼		
1875	32S	63W	30	SE¼	160	1,000
1875	32S	63W	31	SE¼	160	700
1875	32S	63W	30	NE¼	160	750
1875	31S	64W	31	SW¼	160	1,200
1875	34S	63W	3	N½ of NE¼	160	800
				N½ of NW¼		
1875	34S	63W	2	SE¼	160	430
1875	34S	63W	2	S½ of NE¼	160	530
				S½ of NW¼		
1876	32S	62W	4	W½ of SE¼	.80	500
1876	34S	63W	3	SE¼	160	325
1876	34S	63W	3	All	1,280	7,120
			2	All		
1876	34S	63W	3	SW¼	160	640
1876	34S	63W	3	S½ of ¼	160	480
				S½ of NE¼		
1876	32S	62W	4	W½ of SE¼	120	1,200
				SE¼ of SE¼		
1876	33S	63W	27	W½ of NE¼	160	1,120

233

Year	Township	Range	Section	Parts of Sections	No. of Acres	Sales Price
1876	33S	63W	6	Part	80	200
1877	31S	65W	25	Part	160	800
			10	N½ of NE¼		
			3	S½ of SE¼		
1877	32S	68W	31	W½ of SW¼	160	400
				W½ of NW¼		
1877	33S	63W	4	Part	160	400
			9	Part		
1877	34S	63W	3	Part	156	500
1877	34S	63W	2	N½ of NE¼	160	500
				N½ of NW¼		
1878	34S	64W	1	NE¼ of NE¼	160	1,000
				W½ of NE¼		
				NE¼ of NW¼		
1878	33S	63W	18	NW¼	160	1,870
1878	32S	62W	27	SW¼ of NE¼	120	1,000
				N½ of SE¼		
1878	33S	63W	13	E½ of NE¼	80	600
1879	32S	68W	31	W½ of SW¼	320	800
				W½ of NW¼		
			19	SW¼ of NW¼		
				W½ of SW¼		
				NW¼ of NW¼		
1879	33S	63W	36	W½	1,600	17,480
			25	SW¼		
			26	Part		
			27	SE¼		
			34	SE¼		
1880	30S	50W	28	S½ of NW¼	160	300
				NE¼ of NW¼		
			21	SE¼ of SW¼		
1881	32S	63W	20	S½ of NE¼	80	240
1881	34S	63W	4	All	1,600	1,600
			5	All		
			10	NW¼		
				SE¼		
1881	33S	64W	4	SE¼	1,120	1,052
				E½ of SW¼		
	32S	66W		SW¼ of SW¼		
			9	NW¼ of NW¼		
		68W	31	W½ of SW¼		
				W½ of NW¼		
				SE¼ of NE¼		
				NE¼ of SE¼		
			32	SW¼ of NW¼		
				NW¼		
				SW¼ of NW¼		

234

Year	Township	Range	Section	Parts of Sections	No. of Acres	Sales Price
			19	W½ of SW¼		
			30	NW¼ of NW¼		
	33S	63W	6	SW¼		
1881	32S	63W	34	N½ of NW¼	400	1,000
			26	W½ of NW¼		
				NE¼ of NW¼		
			20	S½ of NE¼		
				N½ of SE¼		
		62W	18	NE¼ of SW¼		
1881	33S	68W	30	NW¼ of NE¼	160	400
				NE¼ of SW¼		
				E½ of NW¼		
1881	33S	63W	29	NW¼	160	1,000
1882	34S	64W	1	SE¼ of NE¼	120	4,000
				E½ of SE¼		
1882	33S	62W	28	¼	320	6,000
			22	NW¼ of SE¼		
				E½ of SW¼		
				SW¼ of SW¼		
1882	34S	60W	3	E½ of SW¼	160	300
				SE¼ of NW¼		
				SW¼ of NE¼		
1882	33S	60W	23	SW¼ of NE¼	160	290
				W½ of SW¼		
			22	SE¼ of NE¼		
1882	32S	62W	4	E½ of NE¼	80	600
1882	32S	61W	34	E½ of NE¼	160	1,000
				NW¼ of NE¼		
			35	NW¼ of NW¼		
1882	35S	60W	7	Part	168	300
			18	Part		
1882	32S	66W	27	Part	160	450
1882	33S	62W	33	Part	170	250
1882	33S	60W	14	E½ of SW¼	160	225
				SW¼ of SW¼		
			23	NW¼ of NW¼		
1882	33S	60W	27	SE¼ of SE¼	160	325
			34	E½ of NE¼		
				SW¼ of NE¼		
1882	34S	50W	23	S½ of SW¼	160	300
				SW¼ of SE¼		
			26	NW¼ of NE¼		
1882	34S	50W	35	E½ of SE¼	160	300
				NW¼ of SE¼		
				SW¼ of NE¼		
1882	33S	50W	30	E½ of SW¼	160	275
				SE¼ of NW¼		
				SW¼ of NE¼		
1882	29S	50W	26	W½ of NE¼	160	375
				NE¼ of NE¼		
			25	NW¼ of NW¼		
1882	29S	49W	1	N½ of NW¼	120	300
			2	NW¼ of NW¼		

235

	Year	Township	Range	Section	Parts of Sections	No. of Acres	Sales Price
	1882	29S	44W	28	N½ of NE¼	160	250
					SE¼ of NE¼		
				27	SW¼ of NW¼		
	1883	33S	64W	4	NE¼	160	800
	1883	30S	51W	25	NE¼ of NW¼	160	300
					N½ of NW¼		
					NW¼ of SW¼		
	1883	34S	61W	17	NW¼ of NE¼	160	200
				8	W½ of SE¼		
					NE¼ of SE¼		
	1883	34S	61W	20	E½ of NW¼	160	200
					E½ of SW¼		
	1883	34S	61W	35	S½ of NW¼	160	300
					NW¼ of NW¼		
				26	SW¼ of SW¼		
	1883	34S	61W	27	SE¼	160	300
	1883	32S	54W	1	SE¼ of NE¼	160	300
					E½ of SE¼		
				12	NE¼ of NE¼		
	1883	30S	63W	20	SW¼ of NE¼	160	500
					NW¼ of SE¼		
					E½ of SE¼		
	1883	33S	60W	35	W½ of NW¼	160	300
					NW¼ of SW¼		
				34	NE¼ of SE¼		
236	1883	34S	60W	34	S½ of SE¼	160	285
					SE¼ of SW¼		
				3	NE¼ of NW¼		
	1883	34S	62W	25	E½ of NE¼	160	200
				24	E½ of SE¼		
	1883	32S	68W	19	SW¼ of SW¼	160	725
				30	NE¼ of NW¼		
					W½ of NE¼		
	1883	34S	61W	26	SE¼	160	200
	1883	30S	58W	28	E½ of SW¼	160	300
					NW¼ of SE¼		
					SW¼ of NE¼		
	1883	33S	61W	3	SE¼ of NE¼	160	4,050
					S½ of NW¼		
					SW¼ of NE¼		
	1883	30S	50W	2	W½ of NE¼	160	3,050
					E½ of NW¼		
	1883	30S	50W	2	SW¼ of SW¼	160	300
				10	SE¼ of SE¼		
					N½ of NE¼		
	1883	32S	58W	5	SW¼ of NE¼	160	275
					W½ of SE¼		
					SE¼ of SE¼		
	1883	30S	63W	21	Part	160	700
	1883	30S	42W	4	Part	160	275
				5	Part		

Year	Township	Range	Section	Parts of Sections	No. of Acres	Sales Price
1883	30S	55W	9	SE¼ of NE¼	320	2,000
			10	SW¼ of NW¼		
				W½ of SW¼		
			4	E½ of SW¼		
				SW¼ of SE¼		
			9	NW¼ of NE¼		
1883	30S	42W	1	Part	160	250
			2	Part		
1883	33S	63W	31	NE¼	160	4,000
1883	33S	63W	32	NE¼	160	4,000
1883	33S	64W	30	Part	160	300
1883	33S	62W	28	Part	160	200
1883	30S	55W	9	Part	320	1,000
			10	Part		
			4	Part		
1883	28S	46W	6	W½ of NW¼	160	300
				SE¼ of NW¼		
				SW¼ of NE¼		
1883	30S	42W	2	S½ of NW¼	160	325
				NW¼ of NW¼		
			3	NE½ of NE½		
1883	30S	42W	4	W½ of NE¼	160	300
				NW¼ of SE¼		
				NE¼ of SE¼		
1883	29S	41W	32	Part	160	350
			33	Part		
1883	30S	41W	6	Part	160	325
1883	28S	47W	1	Part	120	400
			2	Part		
1883	28S	48W	3	Part	160	300
1883	28S	47W	5	Part	120	300
1883	33S	64W	2	Part	160	125
			11	Part		
1883	29S	57W	18	NE¼	160	300
1883	34S	63W	6	NE¼	160	4,000
1883	34S	63W	6	SE¼	160	4,000
1883	34S	63W		SE¼	160	4,000
1883	40S	51W	13	SE¼ of SW¼	160	300
				W½ of SW¼		
			24	NE¼ of NW¼		
1884	30S	65W	25	NE¼ of NW¼	160	3,000
				NW¼ of NE¼		
			24	SE¼ of SW¼		
				SW¼ of SE¼		
1886	30S	51W	13	SE¼ of SW¼	1,240	5,500
				SW¼ of SE¼		
			24	NE¼ of NW¼		
				NW¼ of NE¼		
		50W	2	SW¼ of SW¼		

237

Year	Township	Range	Section	Parts of Sections	No. of Acres	Sales Price
			3	SE¼ of SE¼		
			10	N½ of NE¼		
			2	W½ of NE¼		
				E½ of NW¼		
			21	E½ of NW¼		
				N½ of NE¼		
		51W	25	NE¼ of NW¼		
				NW¼ of NW¼		
				SW¼ of NW¼		
				NW¼ of SW¼		
		50W	28	E½ of SW¼		
				NW¼ of SE¼		
				SW¼ of NE¼		
				S½ of NW¼		
				NE¼ of NW¼		
			21	SE¼ of SW¼		
	29S	50W	35	W½ of SE¼		
				SE¼ of SW¼		
1887	34S	42W	22	NW¼ of NW¼	160	5,000
			21	N½ of NE¼		
				NE¼ of NW¼		
1887	32S	43W	16	SW¼ of NE¼	160	10,000
				SE¼ of NE¼		
				NE¼ of SW¼		
				NW¼ of SE¼		
1888	33S	52W	31	SW¼	440	2,000
			32	SW¼ of SW¼		
			31	E½ of SE¼		
				NW¼ of SE¼		
	34S	48W	35	E½ of SE¼		
1888	31S	65W	25	E½ of SE¼	160	5,000
				SW¼ of SW¼		
				SE¼ of SW¼		
1888	32S	44W	13	NE¼	160	1,500
1888	33S	42W	26	SW¼	160	865
1888	33S	41W	20	SE¼	160	1,300
1889	32S	42W	31	SE¼	160	1,000
1889	32S	42W	3	NE¼	160	300
1874	33S	63W	25	W½	12,800	25,000
			36	W½		

All of sections 5, 8, 7, 18, 19, 20, 21, 22, 23, 26, 27, and 34.

		64W		All of sections 13 and 24		
	32S	63W	13	W½		
			28	E½		

E½ of sections 32, 22, 23, 24, 27, and 33.

SANTA FE COUNTY, NEW MEXICO

1887   Book No. F   Page No. 78   Sales Price $500.00

...un pedazo de tierra situado en el Alto llanado La Joya, en
el precinto numero 4 de dicha Condado de Santa Fe, cuyo
pedazo de tierra consta de docientos diez (210) varas de larga
y ciento quince (115) de ancho--cuyos linderos son los
siguientes: por el oriente con el Camino Real que pasa a
Galisteo--por el poniente con tierras de Luis Lovato--por
el Norte con tierras de Juan Manuel Rodriguez--y por el sur
con tierras de los Seguras...

...this piece of land measures 210 varas in length and 115
varas in width--its boundaries are: on the east by the
Camino Real that passes to Galisteo--on the west by lands of
Luis Lovato--on the North by lands of Juan Manuel Rodriguez--
and on the south with lands of the Seguras...

TAOS, NEW MEXICO

L*&&
1877   Book No. A-4   Page No. 123   Sale Price $2,000.00

...toda aqualla porcion y pedazo de tierra quedandose y hallan-
dose en el condado de Taos en el Territorio de Nuevo Mejico,
lindado por el norte por la acequia de Jose Rafael Vigil y el
Rio del Pueblo, por el Oriente por las tierras y propriedad de
Jose de la Cruz Mondragon y Benigno Valdez, por el sur por
el camino que corre del pueblo de los Indios por la plaza de la
loma hasta los Ranchos de Taos, y por el poniente por las
tierras de Mariano de Jesus Lucero, Maria de la Luz Lucero...

...that portion of land situated in Taos County--bounded on the
north by the irrigation ditch of Jose Rafael Vigil and the Rio
del Pueblo River, on the east by the lands and property of
Jose de la Cruz Mondragon y Benigno Valdez, on the south by
the road that runs from the Indian Pueblo through town by
way of the plaza from the hill to Ranchos de Taos, on the west
by the lands of Mariano de Jesus Lucero, Maria de la Luz Lucero...

SANTA FE COUNTY, NEW MEXICO

1882   Book No. L   Page No. 293   Sales Price ᵽ250.00

...en una parte de aqualla mercéd de terreno llamada La Merced
de La Mesita de Juana Lopez situada en el condado de Santa Fe
territorio de Nuevo Mejico donada y consedida por el Govierno
Espanol de España el dia 18 de Tenero de 1782 a Domingo Romero
Miguel Ortiz y Manuel Ortiz y aprobada el dia 29 de noviembre
de 1782. Como queda en los registros y archivos en la oficina
del agrimensor general del Territorio de nuevo Mejico, bajo el
numero 64 haviendo sido confirmado por el Congreso de los
Estados Unidos el dia 28 de enero de 1879 siendo los limites y
linderos de dicha merced de la Mesita de Juana Lopes como sigue
por el norte el filo de la Mesita de Juana Lopez--por el oriente
la linea de los terrenos antiguamente de los Ortegas--por el
sur penias escarpadas y bolsas--por el poniente sierras antiguamente de Juan Antonio Fernandez y Penasco Blanco dicha
partes de la primera parte...

...that certain grant of land known as La Merced de La Mesita
de Juana Lopez, situated in Santa County, New Mexico Territory,
conceded by the Spanish Government to Domingo Romero Miguel
Ortiz y Manuel Ortiz on January 18, 1782..and approved on
November 29, 1782...having been confirmed by the Congress of
the U. S. on January 28, 1879...its boundaries are as follows:
on the north the edge of the Mesita de Juana Lopez--on the east
the line of the lands previously owned by the Ortegas--on the
south sharp boulders and pockets--on the west by mountains
previously owned by Juan Antonio Fernandez and a white cliff...

240

SANTA FE COUNTY, NEW MEXICO

1880   Book No. K   Page No. 248   Sales Price $6,000.00

...toda de la siguiente descrito sitio de tierra, estando y siendo
situada, en el Condado de Santa Fe, en el Territorio de Nuevo
Mejico, y siendo una porcion, de lo que es conocida, como la
Merced de Roque Levato, segun designado en el mapa de la misma,
en la Oficina del Agrimensor General del Territorio de Nuevo
Mejico, a saber comensando en un punto donde hay una mafonera
de piedra puesta al norte 30° al oriente, tres y sesenta y seis
sentimas (3.66) cadenas de la esquina noroeste de la dicha merced
del dicho Roque Lovato y de alli, al norte 10° al este siguiendo
el lado oriental del camino viejo 5'50 cadenas de alli al norte
87° al este 13 cadenas, de alli al norte 48½° al este 4.50
cadenas de alli al norte 50¼° al este 28 cadenas a la esquina
noroeste donde se halle una mafonera de piedra, de alli al
sur 66°, al este 57.50 cadenas a una mafonera de piedra en el
camino viejo 30.00 cadenas de alli al norte 86° al oeste 13.50
cadenas de alli al norte 54° al oeste 5.50 cadenas de alli al
norte 84° al oeste 9.00 cadenas, de alli al sur 41° al oeste
2.26 cadenas al punto de comienzo queda excetada el Campo Santo
en el terreno, juntamente con todo y singular las tenencias
herencias y pertenencias...

All the following described property situated in Santa Fe County,
New Mexico Territory-this land known as the Merced de Roque Lovato
as designated on a map in the office of the Surveyor General of
the New Mexico Territory-described as follows: beginning at a
point where is situated a monument of rocks, situated N30 to the E.,
3.66 chains from the NW corner of the said Merced De Roque Lovato-
from there N 10° to the East following the Eastern side of the
old road 5'50 chains from there 87° North to the East 13 chains.
From there 48½° to the East 4.50 chains from there North 50¼ to
the East 28 chains to the NW corner where is found a rock monument on the road that forms the East boundary of the said Merced.
The said rock monument being the NE corner of the piece of land
passing from there south 41° to the West following the old road
30.00 chains from there North 86° to the West 13.50 chains from
there to the North 54° to the West 5.50 chains from there North
39° to the West 2.00 chains from there 33° to the West 10.00
chains, from there North 84° to the West 9.00 chains, from there
South 41° to the West 2.26 chains to the point of beginning,
excepting the cemetery on the property...

241

RECORD OF SALES OF LAND GRANTS AND ESTATES (OR
SALES OF INTERESTS IN GRANTS). THE SALES ARE
RECORDED IN, AND HERE TRANSLATED FROM, SPANISH

NO.	NAME OF GRANT OR GENERAL LOCATION OF PROPERTY	YEAR OF SALE	BOOK	PAGE	NO. OF ACRES	SALES PRICE ψ	PRICE PER ACRE
1	ranch about 5 miles east of the town of Galisteo in Santa Fe County	1854	B	185	about 2500	1271	.50
2	Land in Las Animas County, Colorado	1887	4	10	1917	8544	4.45
3	Canon de Chama Grant, Rio Arriba County	1886	B	665	2500	300	.12
4	Francisco Montes Vigil Grant, Rio Arriba Co.	1886	B	618	10313	1666	.16
5	Sebastian Martin Land Grant, lying in Taos & Rio Arriba Counties	1881	7	6	51388	250000	4.86
6	Ignacio Chavez Grant, lying in Valencia & Bernalillo Counties	1881	N	101	243036	97000	.40
7	Pedro Sanchez Grant, Bernalillo County	1879	O	381	31803	16000	.51
8	tract of land in Las Lagunitas, Bernalillo County	1882	R	425	160	533	33.34
9	Santa Teresa de Jesus land grant; Bosque Grande land grant; both in Bernalillo County	1887	9	74	6886	2500	.36

242

NO.	NAME OF GRANT OR GENERAL LOCATION OF PROPERTY	YEAR OF SALE	BOOK	PAGE	NO. OF ACRES	SALES PRICE $	PRICE PER ACRE
10	San Pedro and Canon del Agua Grants, Bernalillo County	1884	1	252	3596	10500	3.00
11	one-half of the Baca Grant, Bernalillo County	1885	4	96	57000	10000	.18
12	in the Canon de San Diego, Bennalillo County	1884	3	72	108	200	1.85
13	situated in the valley of La Jarra in Bernalillo County	1861	D	126	160	500	3.13
14	the Sangre de Cristo Grant, Taos County	1871	E	110	500000	500000	1.00
15	the La Costilla Estate, San Luis Park, Colorado	1871	A	89	500000	62500	.13
16	a grant of land one mile square within the Beaubien Miranda Grant, Mora County	1864	B	28	640	3000	4.68
17	a tract of land in Mora County	1872	3	162	160	300	1.88
18	a piece of land situated on the River Ocate	1868	C	64	60	6000	100.00
19	situated in Santa Fe County	1871	E	603	785	37680	48.00
20	T23N, R13E, NW quarter of section 29, Mora County	1883	B	72	160	300	1.88
21	Known as Stage Station, between Trinidad & Maxwell & registered in Mora County	1869	A	221	2560	5000	1.96

243

NO.	NAME OF GRANT OR GENERAL LOCATION OF PROPERTY	YEAR OF SALE	BOOK	PAGE	NO. OF ACRES	SALES PRICE $	PRICE PER ACRE
22	located on the road between Trinidad and Cimarron, registered in Colfax County	1871	A	223	2560	20000	7.82
23	land known as the Rayado & Cimarron land	1862	A	381	640	3000	4.68
24	T15N, R8E; T14N R8E, in Santa Fe County	1874	P	325	661	500	.75
25	Chilili Grant Bernalillo County	1881	O	378	2500	550	.20
26	situated on the Rio Colorado in San Miguel County	1867	3	194	600	2400	4.00
27	Located in Mora County and Known as the "Comancheros"	1885	C	505	160	300	1.88
28	T16N, R18W, S34, Bernalillo County	1884	2	111	80	1600	20.00
29	T16N, R18W, S28 Bernalillo County	1885	3	115	160	100	.63
30	T8N, R8E, S6, Bernalillo County	1885	2	460	160	1000	6.25
31	T9N, R6E, S36, Bernalillo County	1883	W	432	160	8000	50.00
32	T15N, R18W, S14, Bernalillo County	1884	Z	374	160	8000	50.00

244

AN INQUIRY INTO INDIAN LAND RIGHTS

IN THE AMERICAN SOUTHWEST UNDER SPAIN,

MEXICO, AND THE UNITED STATES, WITH

PARTICULAR REFERENCE TO THE JICARILLA

APACHE AREA OF NORTHEASTERN NEW MEXICO

245

by

DONALD C. CUTTER
PROFESSOR OF SOUTHWESTERN HISTORY
THE UNIVERSITY OF NEW MEXICO

Claimant's Exhibit No. POC-21
Indian Claims Commission Docket No. 22A

247

248

I. INTRODUCTION

The following report is submitted with the purpose of clarifying various aspects of Indian land rights, equities, and ownership in the American Southwest under Spain, Mexico and the United States, with particular regard to the Jicarilla Apache area in northeastern New Mexico.

There is no question as regards the area of Jicarilla Apache aboriginal occupancy and possession, the external boundaries of which having been determined by the Indian Claims Commission in its decision of 26 August 1963, paragraph 60, found on page 30 of Findings of Fact. However, the Commission's Opinion concluded that "all relevant matters concerning Spanish and Mexican land grants both of law and fact, " within the award areas were to be determined at a later hearing.

It is intended to examine herein the nature of claims to such grants before and at United States confirmation), the process of obtaining these grants, the legal formalities of becoming a grantee thereto, the condition of said grants, the type of land usage permitted and/or required thereon, the legal extent of these concessions and the results of Spanish or Mexican land policy upon the aboriginal occupancy of the Jicarilla Apaches. It is therefore pertinent to examine each of the individual grants within the exterior boundaries of the Jicarilla award area as well as Spanish and Mexican land laws in general. Parallel developments in other areas of the Hispanic

Southwest also will be examined, such examination to serve as a basis for comparison and for providing a broader foundation for certain generalizations about the land grant process under the Hispanic sovereigns of the Southwest.

II. SPANISH AND MEXICAN LAND LAWS

A. IN GENERAL

European governments operating colonies in the New World uniformly respected the prior rights of the aborigine to use and occupancy of land. References to this universal respect are to be found in abundance in the historical documentation and interpretation of the period from early contact to mid-19th Century, in decisions of the United States Supreme Court and in juridical literature.

250

The European colonizing nations of the 15th, 16th, 17th and 18th Centuries laid claim by symbolic acts of possession, and other standard forms, to the unpreempted areas of the earth. These claims to exclusive jurisdiction over areas discovered or colonized were in the nature of declarations to other "Christian princes" (i.e., civilized nations) of sovereignty having been established.[1] The United States Supreme Court recognized this principle that discovery gave "to the nation making the discovery the sole right of acquiring the soil from the natives, and establishing settlements upon it. It was a right with which no Europeans could interfere.

---

1. For an admirable discussion of the act of possession, see: Manuel P. Servin, The Act of Sovereignty in the Age of Discovery, Ph.D. dissertation, University of Southern California, 1958.

It was a right which all asserted for themselves, and to the assertion of which, by others, all assented" (emphasis added). [1] Its equal or superior applicability is noted in Hispanic activity in the New World. Torchiana, in his Mission of Santa Cruz (PDC-12), speaking generally about Indian land rights in the Americas, stated: "While the right of the Indians to the land by occupancy and the law of alienation, subject to confirmation by the conquerors, was acknowledged in theory by all the discovering nations in North America - Spain, France, the Netherlands and England - Spain alone remained true to this theory." In Chouteau v. Molony (16 Howard 203 (1853)), the Supreme Court indicated that the aboriginal rights of the Fox Indians in Spanish Louisiana possessed such strong foundation that an alleged grant of lands by the Spanish Governor within the aboriginal Fox holdings was branded "an unaccountable and capricious exercise of official power, contrary to the uniform usage of his predecessors in respect to the sales of Indian lands, and that it could give no property to the grantee. It is not meant, by what has just been said, that the Spanish governors could not relinquish the interest or title of the Crown in Indian lands and for more than a mile square; but when that was done, the grants were made subject to the rights of Indian occupancy. They did not take effect until that occupancy ceased, and whilst it continued it was not in the power of the Spanish governor to authorize any one to interfere with it." (p. 239) The Court had stated earlier in the Decision, at page 236-237, that "We are now

251

---

1. Johnson and Graham's LESSEE v. McIntosh, 8 Wheat. 543 (1823).

speaking of Indian lands, such as these were, and not of those portions of land which were assigned to the Christian Indians for villages and residences, where the Indian occupancy had been abandoned by them, or where it had been yielded by them in a treaty."

The general outline of what was to be the Indian policy of the United States was laid down in the Northwest Ordinance of 13 July 1787 (1. Stat. 50), article 3: "The utmost good faith shall always be observed towards the Indians; their land and property shall never be taken from them without their consent; and in their property, rights and liberty, they never shall be invaded or disturbed, unless in just and lawful wars authorized by Congress: but laws founded in justice and humanity shall from time to time be made, for preventing wrongs from being done to them, and for preserving peace and friendship with them."

252

B. RECOPILACION - A BLANKET OF PROTECTION

Concerning the Indian land status under the Hispanic sovereigns, the great landmark of applicable juridical material is the Recopilacion de Leyes de los Reynos de las Indias (PDC-9), a three volume compilation of decrees concerning the Spanish New World. This great codification was brought forth for better government in the Indies. Particularly applicable as regards the rights of the Indians was Tomo (Volume) Segundo, which "bristled with protection" for the aborigines. In Book IV, title I, the discoverers were enjoined from engaging in wars with the Indians, or of doing them any damage, or of taking their goods, except in trade, or if they should give them up of their free will (law x). Law xii ordered the discoverers to obey the laws of the Recopilacion, and especially those in behalf of the Indians. Book IV, title XII, Law vii, ordered that in distribution of lands that it be done without harm to the Indians. Law ix ordered that lands not be given out in prejudice of the Indians and that those already given out be returned to their owners. Law xii prohibited establishment of major and minor livestock ranchos where they could do damage to the pueblos and crop lands of the Indians. Law xviii required that Indians be allowed lands. Thus under the law of Spain the Indians were protected in their property rights.

There are additional laws dealing with the protection of Indian rights, but in essence these are repetitious in nature. Hubert Howe   253
Bancroft, the pioneer historian and collector of Western Americana, though writing about California,[1] summarized all in a single sentence. "Indian lands in actual use and occupation could not be granted to Spaniards." (pp. 245-246) Concerning land, then, the Spanish government stood in a protective relationship to the Indians and did not betray its trust.

---

1.   Bancroft, California Pastoral (PDC-11)

C. EFFECT OF MEXICAN INDEPENDENCE

At the successful conclusion of the Spanish American Wars for Independence, Mexico won its freedom from Spain. In much the same way that the United States after its independence relied upon English legal precedent, so also did Mexico follow her earlier Hispano-Roman juridical heritage.

The early period of Mexican independence introduces two documents of particular significance. The first is the revolutionary pronouncement of Agustin Iturbide, dated 24 February 1821, known as the Plan of Iguala. It was written as a piece of political propaganda, but it soon became a fixed principle of Mexican law. The effect of the Plan was to elevate the social status of the Indian, who had done much to insure victory in the revolution. In part the Plan provided that "all the inhabitants of New Spain (Mexico), without distinction, whether Europeans, Africans or Indians, are citizens of this monarchy, with the right to be employed in any post according to their merits and virtues." It added that "the person and property of every citizen will be respected and protected by the Government." Thus, added to the earlier protection of Spanish colonial law, the Indians now had full citizenship, a status that they would never lose in Mexican law.

254

The second document from the revolutionary period which is significant is the Treaty of Cordoba. Signed by the last Viceroy of New Spain, the treaty conceded independence to Mexico, 24 August 1821.

D. TREATY OF GUADALUPE-HIDALGO

A quarter of a century later the Indians of New Mexico learned that

there would be yet another change of sovereignty. At the consummation

of the war between the United States and Mexico in 1846-48, the area of

the Southwestern United States, known of as the Mexican Cession, became

a portion of the Union. The definitive treaty, that of Guadalupe-Hidalgo,

with ratifications exchanged at Queretaro, contains provisions bearing on

our questions.

Article VIII
Mexicans now established in territories previously belonging to
Mexico, and which remain for the future within the limits of the
United States, as defined by the present treaty, shall be free to
continue where they now reside, or to remove at any time to
the Mexican republic, retaining the property which they possess
in the said territories, or disposing thereof, and removing the
proceeds wherever they please, without their being subjected,
on this account, to any contribution, tax, or charge whatever.

255

Those who shall prefer to remain in the said territories, may
either retain the title and rights of Mexican citizens, or acquire
those of citizens of the United States. But they shall be under
the obligation to make their election within one year from the
date of the exchange of ratifications of this treaty; and those who
shall remain in the said territories after the expiration of that
year, without having declared their intention to retain the character of Mexicans, shall be considered to have elected to become
citizens of the United States.

In the said territories, property of every kind, now belonging
to Mexicans not established there, shall be inviolably respected.
The present owners, the heirs of these, and all Mexicans who
may hereafter acquire said property by contract, shall enjoy
with respect to it guaranties equally ample as if the same be-
longed to citizens of the United States.

Article IX

Mexicans who, in the territories aforesaid, shall not preserve
the character of citizens of the Mexican republic, conformably
with what is stipulated in the preceding articles, shall be incorporated into the Union of the United States, and be admitted
at the proper time (to be judged of by the Congress of the
United States) to the enjoyment of all the rights of citizens of
the United States, according to the principles of the constitu-
tion; and in the mean time shall be maintained and protected
in the free enjoyment of their liberty and property, and secured
in the free exercise of their religion without restriction.
(U.S. Statutes at Large, Vol. 9, pp. 922 ff.)

"The treaty of Guadalupe Hidalgo recognizes both legal and equitable

rights, and should be administered in a liberal spirit," according to the

opinion of the Supreme Court in United States v. Moreno (1 Wall. 400).

III. UNITED STATES SOVEREIGNTY

A. NO CHANGE IN OWNERSHIP WITH CHANGE IN SOVEREIGNTY

256   The fact that a change of sovereignty did not entail any change in

property ownership had already been established in acquisition of Louisiana

from France in 1803. Though in law this is an undisputed proposition, it

has been confused in popular and even historical thinking. The oft-repeated

national boast that the United States purchased Louisiana for the ridicu-

lously low price of 3/5ths of a cent an acre is inaccurate as regards the

real estate business. The actual fact is that the United States purchased

the right to rule the area. It was merely a monetary consideration paid

to France for the transfer of sovereignty.

Thus the property rights of persons, citizens of Mexico, were not

adversely affected by the transfer of sovereignty from Mexico to the

United States under the terms of the Treaty of Guadalupe-Hidalgo or under earlier precedents. Therefore the Jicarilla Apaches entered the period of United States sovereignty with an expressed guarantee of their property rights.

B. ACQUISITION OF TERRITORY FROM OTHER SOVEREIGNS

Superficially the acquisition of the Mexican Cession of 1848 seems like a unique experience, insofar as it was the first large scale acquisition of territory from Hispanic land holdings. However, such is not the case. In 1803, the Louisiana area was purchased from France, but France had never reasserted full authority over the land. Indeed, it had been under exclusive control of Spain since shortly after the French and Indian War (Seven Years War), concluding with the Peace of Paris of 1763. Speaking of Napoleon's quick sale of Louisiana to the United States, Hafen & Rister aptly expressed the nature of this transaction: "The French chef drew from Europe's English fueled oven the Spanish cake, and with burnt fingers dropped it into the lap of Uncle Sam."[1] But it was essentially a Spanish territory. From this very area emanates one of the strongest Supreme Court statements on the nature of Indian land rights in Chouteau v. Molony (16 Howard 203, 236 (1853)): "It is a fact in the case,

257

---

1. LeRoy R. Hafen and Carl Coke Rister, Western America, p. 171 (Englewood Cliffs, N. J., Prentice Hall, Inc. 1950 (second edition). (PDC-13.)

that the Indian title to the country had not been extinguished by Spain, and

that Spain had not the right of occupancy. The Indians had the right to con-

tinue it as long as they pleased, or to sell out parts of it - the sale being

made conformably to the laws of Spain, and being afterwards confirmed

by the king or his representative, the Governor of Louisiana."

"Apparently the Foxes were as nomadic in their habits as most of

the other Plains tribes, so that the correct historical view would seem

to be that if Spain ever denied title by aboriginal occupancy to certain

Indian tribes, it was because these tribes did not in fact maintain exclu-

sive occupancy of any territory at all but merely wandered over lands

which were traversed by other tribes as well. In this situation even our

own law recognizes that no possessory rights are created. There would

258   seem, therefore, to be no valid reason to suppose that the Spanish law

was more rigorous than the law of Great Britain or the United States with

respect to the recognition of Indian possessory rights derived from abor-

iginal occupancy. We will return to Chouteau v. Molony later in connection

with subsurface rights." (U.S. Department of Interior, Federal Indian

Law, PDC-14.)

IV. DISTRIBUTION OF LAND IN THE SOUTHWEST UNDER SPAIN AND MEXICO

A. IN GENERAL

There were several systems of land distribution in effect at various times. These include pueblo (or town) grants, rancho grants, and empresario concessions. In addition, with particular reference to New Mexico, there was the recognition of pre-existing land use patterns of the Pueblo Indians. These Pueblos de Indios were a matter of formal recognition by the sovereign, Spain, of the occupancy and possession of traditional lands. Herbert O. Brayer, in The University of New Mexico Bulletin, "Pueblo Indian Land Grants of the 'Rio Abajo,' New Mexico," Exhibit PDC-1, outlines the ward and guardian relationship existing between the Indian and the Spanish government (pp. 8-16). Subsequently, Brayer notes: "That the Spanish laws in force previous to 1821, relative to the Pueblo Indian and to the land policy, remained in full force." With the exception of the Pecos Pueblo, the specific areas under consideration by Brayer lie outside the Jicarilla area, but the principles elucidated are valid.

Of the other three types of Hispanic grant, we can eliminate from consideration the empresario type concession (see PDC-13). Though applicable to any portion of the Mexican nation possessing requisite lands, this entrepreneurial system of reward for persons engaged in large scale colonization projects was applied only to the Texas area, as far as areas within the United States are concerned.

259

This leaves two types of potential land systems to be considered, the rancho and the town (sometimes called community) grant. Both are widespread throughout the Southwest area, and there is no significant difference in their operation whether the area discussed by New Mexico, Arizona, Texas or California. Professor John Walton Caughey, in his work <u>California,</u> though speaking of that area specifically, made some generalizations concerning the land grant systems that are quite pertinent.

> In the earliest years Spain had preferred that new settlers reside in the pueblos or near the presidios, but she was ready shortly to make generous grants to prospective ranchers. Two features of these land grants may appall Anglo-Saxons; first, that they conveyed a usufructuary right rather than an absolute title, and second, that they involved such extensive acreage. [1]

B. <u>GRANTS RESTRICTED TO VACANT LAND</u>

260

Under Spanish and Mexican law, it was required that land be <u>vacant</u> before it could be granted to individual or collective grantees.[2]   Under the terms of the Mexican Colonization Law of 1828 (PDC-4): Article 1st. "The governors (gefes politicos) of the territories are authorized (in compliance with the law of the general Congress of the 18th of August, 1824,

---

1.   John Walton Caughey, <u>California</u> (New York, Prentice Hall, Inc., 1940) p. 197 (PDC-10).
2.   Exhibit PDC-3, Hon. William W. Morrow, <u>Spanish and Mexican Private Land Grants,</u> is the evaluation by a United States Circuit Court of Appeals Judge. On page 16 he indicates the need for the land to be vacant and whether it could be granted without injury to third persons or the public.

and under the conditions hereafter specified) to grant vacant lands /italics mine7 in their respective territories to such contractors (empresarios) families, or private persons, whether Mexicans or foreigners, who may ask for them, for the purpose of cultivating and inhabiting them." Under the contingency that there was Indian occupation of a portion of a proposed grant: "This was the theory: when a grant was made of land upon which was a rancheria, or Indian settlement, such a grant was made subject to the rights of the Indian, and the grantee did not acquire title or possession until the village, of its own free will, removed from the grant."[1] Expressed differently by Commissioner of Indian Affairs H. Price to the Secretary of the Interior, Washington, January 10, 1884 in 48th Congress, 1st Session, Senate Executive Document 49, he stated in part:

> This work of despoiling the Indians has been done /by the United States7 under the forms of law, but, as is believed, in violation of the terms of the law and of the stipulation contained in the original grants. By the fundamental laws of the Mexican Republic of 1824, the regulation of 1828, and the regulation of the departmental legislature, one condition was that in making private grants of lands, the lands granted must be vacant lands. Lands occupied by and in possession of Indians were not such vacant land, for by the same laws and regulations it was provided that such grants must be without prejudice or damage to the Indians, and that such land granted to the damage and injury of the Indians should be returned to the rightful owners. (U.S. Govt. Docs. Serial 2162.)

261

---

1.   Hubert Howe Bancroft, California Pastoral, p. 246 (PDC-11).

C. PHYSICAL LIMITS OF GRANTS

The above quotation draws our attention to the Mexican laws concerning the granting of land to rancho grantees. Whereas Spain had made but few grants of land, and these were relatively much smaller than the later grants, Mexico placed a physical limit on the land to be embraced within a grant. The various conditions governing land and colonization are contained in translation in Exhibit PDC-4, John A. Rockwell, A Compilation of Spanish and Mexican Law in Relation to Mines, and Titles to Real Estate, Vol. I, published in New York, 1851. Two specific decrees are pertinent: 1) the decree of 18th August, 1824, respecting colonization, and 2) general rules and regulations for the colonization of territories of the republic of Mexico, November 21, 1828.

The former provided that those territories comprised within twenty leagues of the boundaries of any foreign nation, or within ten leagues of the seacoast, cannot be colonized without the previous approval of the supreme general executive power and that "No one person shall be allowed to obtain the ownership of more than one league square, of five thousand varas (5,000 v.) of irrigable land (de regadio), four superficial ones of land dependent on the seasons (de temporal), and six superficial ones for the purpose of rearing cattle (de abreradiso)." Thus by the terms of this colonization decree the maximum possible land holding was 11 leagues of land. See also Exhibits PDC-6 and PDC-7. The Supreme Court agrees completely in United States v. Maxwell Land Grant Co. (121 U.S. 325, 360-361, 30 L. ed. 949): "It has been repeatedly decided by this court that it was the practice of the government of Mexico under that article /F12 of the Colonization Law of 1824/, to limit its grants of public lands in the Territories to eleven square leagues for each individual."

The second of the two decrees indicates that the land must be vacant, as indicated above. It also provides, in Section 2, that the petitioner for a land grant must describe "as distinctly as possible, by means of a map, the land asked for." Section 3 calls for the governor to obtain the necessary information whether the petition embraces the requisite conditions demanded by said law of the 18th of August /1824/, both as regards the land and the candidate, in order that the petitioner may at once be attended to; or if it be preferred, the respective municipal authority may be consulted, whether there be any objection to making the grant or not. Further pertinent provisions are:

263

"4th. This being done, the governor will accede or not to such a petition, in exact conformity to the laws on the subject, and especially to the before-mentioned one of the 18th of August, 1824.

"5th. The grants made to families or private persons shall not be held to be definitely valid without the previous consent of the territorial deputation, to which end the respective documents (espedientes) shall be forwarded to it.

"6th. When the governor shall not obtain the approbation of the territorial deputation, he shall report to the supreme government, forwarding the necessary documents for its decision.

"8th. The definitive grant asked for being made, a document signed by the governor shall be given, to serve as a title to the party interested, wherein it must be stated that said grant is made in exact conformity with the provisions of the laws in virtue whereof possession shall be given.

"9th. The necessary record shall be kept in a book destined for the purpose, of all the petitions presented, and grants made, with the maps of the lands granted, and the circumstantial report shall be forwarded quarterly to the supreme government."

D. TOWN GRANTS

A different type of grant was the town or pueblo grant. This was largely a communal type of ownership, with certain land being distributed to individuals and certain rights being held in community.[1] These grants, exclusive of pasture and woodlands, were limited by law to 4 leagues of land, measured in a square or oblong form from the center of the community. The Recopilacion (PDC-9), Book IV, Title 5, LAW 6, clearly indicates this four league maximum, outside of which the land was open to all citizens who chose to use it, never becoming private property. A propos of land measurements, there was some confusion by the U.S. Surveyor General of New Mexico soon after 1848 concerning the league as a measure. However, it ought to have been clear then, as it is now, that a league was both a linear measure of approximately 2.8 miles, and an areal measure consisting of about 4,400 acres.

264

---

1. See Espinosa, "New Mexico Land Grants," PDC-15; see also D-68.

E. GRANT MEASUREMENTS

In New Mexico described boundaries petitioned by potential grantees to Spanish or Mexican sovereigns sometimes exceeded the eleven league maximum for private grants. In other words, imprecise boundary descriptions in grant petitions did not measure an exact eleven leagues. Maps were frequently left unmade because of the difficult nature of the terrain, and general boundaries of areas to be granted were substituted for the more specific rules enforced elsewhere in the Mexican republic. But this indefiniteness did not give the grantee a claim to any more than the maximum land which could be embraced in a single grant. Judge Morrow in his admirable work <u>Spanish and Mexican Private Land Grants</u> (PDC-3) lends clarity to the matter: "The authority to make a grant to individuals was given to the Governors of the territories, to the extent of eleven square leagues, or 48,712.4 acres." He later adds: "The grants in New Mexico, like those in California, were generally located within exterior boundaries embracing a much larger area than the grant called for in square leagues." These grants were known of as "floating grants," and as the pressure for lands increased there was frequently a second claimant requesting the surplus portion, or <u>sobrante</u> area. Such a second claim would force an election on the part of the original grantee, and would permit creation of a second grant within the same external boundaries, but exclusive of the area of the first grant. In certain portions of the Spanish

265

Southwest, particularly California, this existence of a <u>sobrante</u>, or surplus, especially when no second Hispanic claimant appeared, invited later homestead and preemption claims by persons claiming land under the laws of the United States. To avoid such a possibility in the case of New Mexico, Congress prohibited entry by U.S. claimants on the areas inside the exterior boundaries of the Hispanic land claims, even though these areas were immodestly in excess of the permissible eleven league maximum.

F. PROBLEMS OF NEW MEXICO LAND GRANTS

Historian-lawyer William A. Keleher, in his <u>Maxwell Land Grant</u>, portions of which are presented as Exhibit PDC-5, discusses the nature of these excessive claims, and indicates that the responsibility therefor is largely chargeable to the U.S. Government. "The land grant title of New Mexico for decades had been locked up in pigeon holes either in the office of the Surveyor General in Santa Fe, in the office of the Secretary of the Interior in Washington, or in the desk of some committee member of Congress in the Capitol building...(p. 8)" New Mexico Territorial Governor Lionel A. Shelton asserted: "Confirmations have been carelessly made and it is generally believed that errors and frauds have been practiced and apparently legalized through want of knowledge of or attention to the subject. Grants have been confirmed of greater dimensions than the Spanish or Mexican laws seem to justify, and though mineral lands were not alienated in fee simple by those governments,

266

still confirmatory acts have been passed and patents issued, under which

it is claimed that minerals pass to patentees. Success in securing con-

firmation of grants of a doubtful character so encouraged and emboldened

the covetous that it is alleged the manufacture of grant papers became an

occupation, and surveys have been erroneously made as to lead to a be-

lief that these grants are endowed with India rubber qualities."

(Keleher, p. 9)

Another New Mexico Territorial Governor, Edmund G. Ross, com-

mented on the illegalities concerning these boundaries:

> So common has this practice become of enlarging the
> boundaries of bona fide grants made by Spain and
> Mexico, and so general and apparently well grounded
> is the suspicion that there has been in operation for
> many years a systematic and cunningly executed
> scheme for the manufacture of fraudulent titles to
> large tracts of public domain under the guise of Spanish
> and Mexican grants, that the public faith in all such
> titles has largely diminished. (Keleher, p. 10)

267

V. THE PATENTED AREAS WITHIN THE JICARILLA CLAIM

There yet remains the applicability of the aforementioned laws,

decrees and interpretations to the area embraced within the exterior

boundaries of the Jicarilla Claim. A good number of these patented areas

present irregularities, demonstrating great variance from the accepted

norms.

A. THE MAXWELL GRANT

Exhibit PDC-5, entitled Maxwell Land Grant, written by lawyer

William A. Keleher, concerns this concession. This Grant was made to ex-Canadian Charles Beaubien and Guadalupe Miranda, with the purpose of dividing it between them. At most it might have contained 22 leagues (11 for each grantee), or approximately 98,000 acres. As regards size, however, Beaubien, one of the original grantees admitted that "the grant does not exceed fifteen or eighteen (leagues)." (Private Land Claims in New Mexico, D-67, p. 249). Keleher asserts (p. 29) that it is doubtful if the next owner, Lucien Maxwell, had the faintest conception of what its eventual acreage might contain, "being under the impression probably for many years that it contained between 32,000 and 97,424 acres, or twenty-two Spanish leagues." It was only after U. S. sovereignty in the Southwest that the area was magnified to 1,714,764.93 acres. Keleher states that the Indians continued in de facto possession of the land well into the American period, without knowing that there was any adverse claim to their hunting and fishing areas (Keleher, p. 30). Even as late as the Civil War period, the Indians were still resident on the Maxwell Grant (p. 51). The Supreme Court, lacking solid information on the nature of Spanish colonization requirements, considered this to be an empresario grant, but there is no evidence that any of the formalities for obtaining this type of a concession were ever formally entered into with the Mexican central government, or that the provisions of such con-cessions were ever carried out. See: Mexican Colonization Laws of 1824 and 1828 (PDC-4).

Concerning this and other grants, the New Mexico claimants to land when presenting their claims purposely concealed the nature of

Indian rights in those lands. It also appears that these Indian rights and
equities were of little interest to the United States Surveyor General for
New Mexico. Though a rather lengthy set of instructions were provided
for the U.S. Surveyor General, the rights of the Jicarilla Apaches and
other Tribes were not considered. (For these instructions see Exhibit
PDC-7). The Indian occupants of the land, including that which was being patented in excess of Mexican law governing land grants, did not receive any sort of hearing, nor did their guardian (the United States) speak
for them.

B. SANGRE DE CRISTO GRANT
(D-67, pp.

This grant made to Narciso Beaubien and Luis Lee exceeded in area
the acreage applied for and the acreage authorized under Mexican law: 269

> The area patented by the United States was about
> 270,000 acres, when the original grant documents
> presented before the Surveyor General called for
> one sitio (one league) for each of the two grantees.
> See: Private Land Claims documents, esp. p. 531.
> Thus the total allowable amount would be 4,400
> acres or 8,800 acres depending on the interpreta-
> tion of the first objection.

The pertinent quotation for the above objection follows:

> ..... That desiring to encourage the agriculture of
> the country in such a way that it may come to be in
> a flourishing condition, and finding our lands too
> small to accomplish it, we have seen and examined
> with sufficient care that which the rivers Costilla,
> Culebra, and Trinchera embrace, the Rito (little
> river), de los Indios, and Sangre de Cristo included,
> as far as their confluence with the Rio del Norte,

and finding in it the qualities of fruitfulness, fertile
lands for cultivation, abundant pastures and waters,
and all that is required for its settlement and the
raising of the larger kinds of stock and sheep.
Satisfied of all this, and that they are vacant public
lands, we have not hesitated to apply to your excel-
lency, praying that you will deign as an act of justice
to grant to us in that said tract of land the possession
of one sitio (one square league) of lands to each....

C. PUEBLO DE SAN CRISTOVAL TRACT (E. W. EATON)
(D-67, pp. 484-512)

Though the granting procedures here are somewhat hard to follow,

it is clear that the grant was never at any time, by any stretch of the

rules, intended to cover the 81,000 approximate acres patented in 1879.

In 1853 the land was sold to Eaton in a sheriff's sale. It had been orig-

inally granted to Domingo Fernandez, and conveyed in 1851 to Alexander

270   W. Reynolds and E. W. Eaton. The land involved was described as:

A certain ranch lying and being in the County of Santa Fe, Territory of

New Mexico, about five miles east of Galisteo, containing about 2,500

acres, more or less, with about 50 acres of the same in good cultiva-

tion....." Private Land Claims, p. 507.

D. BISHOP JOHN LAMY GRANT
(D-67, pp. 154-163)

Patented at some 16,500 acres, there seems to be no question about

this. It was clearly recognized by the prior sovereign, and appears valid,

though no original grant papers were produced.

E. TECOLOTE GRANT
(D-67, pp. 98-104)

1) The original grantees were run off by the Indians about 1829 or 1839.

2) According to their own documents 'in the case they indicate that: "said grant has never been surveyed, and no plat of the same can therefore be furnished, but they think that said grant is about three miles from north to south, and about four miles from east to west;" which would mean that the grantees considered it to be a 12 sq. mi. area, or 7,680 acres. It was patented by the U.S. for over 48,000 acres.

3) Apparently it was not a recognized town, since the attorney for the Tecolote claim said: "The town of Tecolote is not an incorporated town. See: Private Land Claims, pp. 288-294.

F. DONANCIANO VIGIL or LOS TRIGOS
(D-67, pp. 105-154)

This grant area was subject to dual claim. It contained between 9,000 and 13,000 acres. It appears to be valid on the basis of Mexican recognition. A few points are worthy of mention:

271

1) Indian rights are considered in the original 1815 grant which was made "with the condition that they shall not interfere with the Indians nor the inhabitants of El Bado, and the further condition that they shall not disturb anyone in the pastures or watering places which are common..."

2) The Indians of Pecos Pueblo were respected in their pueblo rights by being permitted to measure their 5,000 vara (one league) ownership in the direction of Los Trigos.

3) The area was abandoned in 1829 because of Indian hostility, Private Land Claims, pp. 295-344.

G. ANTON CHICO
(D-68, pp. 138-152)

This appears to be a standard town situation which should automatically have the regular approximately 18,000 acre limitation. Any lands beyond this would have been communal, and not subject to private ownership. Even within the 4 league area, lands were not in the same fee simple relationship of Anglo law. Noteworthy at Anton Chico is the fact that the original settlers were run off by the Indians at an unspecified date, and that some returned to become settlers in the 1834 redistribution of land. As in other town grants the pastures and watering places were to be held in common. It is to be noted that this grant encroaches on the Preston Beck claim and vice versa.

272

H. PRESTON BECK (OJITO DE LAS GALLINAS)
(D-66, pp. 440-476)

The size of this grant is in excess of the maximum permitted. Moreover, there is an interruption in holding the land caused by local Indian hostility. Obtained by Beck in the territorial period and patented for an excessive amount of about 320,000 acres, it should have been no more than a maximum grant of about 48,000 acres.

I. ALEXANDER VALLE GRANT
(D-67, pp. 279-294)

This is a grant of modest dimensions. Though there seem to be some irregularities, such as lack of precision in size and lack of clarity of title transfer, the grant seems valid for its approximate 1,000 acres.

Notable features of the case include:

1) The area requested "is situate in the vicinity of the Pecos Pueblo, to the west, beyond the limits of the Pueblo, as is well known by the protector of the Indians and the alcalde of that jurisdiction, both of whom are aware that our petition is not in prejudice to a third person nor to the Indians of that district (republica in the original)..."

2) Protector of the Indians Felipe Sandoval certified that the land was at "a regular distance and entirely separated from the possession of said pueblo..."

3) The acting governor ordered the First Alcalde to "measure the pieces (suertes) of tillable land, limiting the grants solely to the land they plough and plant, with the obligation that they shall enclose the same to prevent the recovery of damages because the grounds (terrenos, i.e., lands) must be common and public pastures for the Indians and citizens that have a right therein." See: Private Land Claims, pp. 471-73.

273

J. JOSE L. PEREA GRANT
(D-67, pp. 257-268)

Except for the fact that Perea, the elder, came into possession of his lands by squatting on them for a period of nine years prior to asking official recognition of his claim, everything about this claim is in order. He asked for and received 4 leagues of land; the U.S. Surveyor General for New Mexico determined that this was so and the area was patented in the amount of about 19,000 acres. There was an indication that the Indians were in actual possession of the area, since the claimant indicated that occupation was not continuous, "from the time of said grant up to the present time (confirmation proceedings), having been used for grazing purposes when it could be done with safety from the Indians." See: Private Land Claims, p. 457.

K. SAN MIGUEL DEL BADO GRANT
(D-79, pp. 77-87)

This grant was made to Lorenzo Marquez and over fifty other persons. Since they were not named, though 13 of them were indicated as being Indians, they were not considered to be co-grantees. The area was patented for about 1,500 acres, and though the original limits were not clear, this quantity seems to be in line with reality. See: Private Land Claims, p. 2066.

L. PECOS PUEBLO
(D-66, p. 506)

274

This pueblo grant of four leagues, patented by the U.S. at the appropriate pueblo figure of 18,763 acres, is based on a purported grant of 1689. Governor Domingo Jironza Petroz (sic) de Cruzate, in an effort to maintain the friendship of certain Indian groups during the reconquest of New Mexico following the Pueblo Revolt of 1680, supposedly issued a series of grants. The following boundaries are indicated: "On the north one league, and on the east one league, and on the west one league, and on the south one league, and these four lines to be measured from the four corners of the pueblo (village), leaving out the temple, which is situated at the south of the said pueblo (village)..."

M. ANTONIO ORTIZ GRANT
(D-69, pp. 38-51)

This Spanish period grant was made in 1819. After years of occupation, Ortiz was driven off the land by the Indians, and apparently did not return, nor did his heirs until after the U.S. patented the land. This would seem to indicate Indian use of this land before, during, and after 1846. The United States patented this for 163,000 acres. In 1893 it was alleged that the grant contained 60,000 acres more than was originally claimed. See: Private Land Claims, pp. 892-99.

N. AGUA NEGRA (ANTONIO SANDOVAL)
(D-67, pp. 191-200)

Though only one league of land was originally requested by Sandoval's wife, the grantee was put in possession of one league of 5,000 Castilian varas in each of the four directions from the Agua Negra spring. This would make the grant one of four leagues, or about 17,600 acres. This seems to be in proper form. See: Private Land Claims, pp. 381-390.

O. ARROYO HONDO
(PDC-7)

Only partially embraced within the Jicarilla area, it was granted to a sizeable group. Each person was to receive their plots, and the remainder was to be a commons. The United States divided 18,000 or more acres among the heirs and successors in interest, thereby doing away with the common land. The original grant and act of possession were not produced, nor their absence accounted for. See: Private Land Claims, p. 2528.

P. JOHN SCOLLY ET AL (JUNTA DE LOS RIOS)
(D-67, pp. 163-168)

This was a very late grant in the Mexican period, a matter of only several months before the U.S. invasion of New Mexico. Earlier, members

of the same group had asked for the land in a 10 league grant, but the
time period for taking possession lapsed. In the repetition of request,
the amount was reduced to 5 leagues, with the "condition that the pasture
and watering places shall be held in common, excepting in the centre of
their fields"; and when being put in possession they were warned of the
requirement to cultivate it within five years, on pain of losing the land.
"I made known to them the other conditions required by the laws of possession, such as being forbidden to dispose of the land until it was cultivated by themselves...." Scolly wanted his grant patented for 25 leagues,
as he would have liked to have considered 5 square leagues to have meant;
but the United States, as the Mexican nation before it would have done,
indicated that it was a five league grant. It had originally been requested
as a ten league grant, and had upon subsequent petition been reduced to
five, not increased to twenty five.

276

Q. BACA LOCATION #2
(D-68, pp. 3-45)

This grant is related to the Town of Las Vegas grant. Under any
circumstances, and though this grant appears only slightly larger than the
maximum permissible grant under Hispanic sovereignty, it is a grant in
lieu of some supposed right in land in Las Vegas area. Baca had received
a grant, subsequently reconfirmed, but was run off by the local Indians
(or others). The land was subsequently granted to a group of settlers.
The Baca claim is further complicated by lack of documentary evidence

of Baca ever having been placed in possession. Protest by the Bacas
to adverse possession was delayed until 1848 (though the document was
dated September 20, 1837). Land was granted to Baca elsewhere within
the Jicarilla area. The entire grant is a creation of the United States
period of control. See: Private Land Claims, pp. 847-48 (PDC-7).

R. LAS VEGAS GRANT
(D-68, pp. 3-45)

Connected with the foregoing Baca claim, this was a town grant.
This appears to be a legal town grant. Four leagues, the authorized
town grant stipulated in Book IV, Title V, Law vi, of the Recopilacion
de Leyes de Indias, would seem to be the only area that would be capable
of being reduced to a fee simple ownership. The rest would be pasture
and other common lands. The U.S. patented the area for some 431,000
acres. The grant calls for anyone to have equal rights in the area along
with the original recipients. See: Private Land Claims, pp. 618-19.

277

S. PABLO MONTOYA GRANT
(D-69, pp. 20-27)

Granted in the Mexican period. After some 14 to 15 years of occupation, the claimants were driven from the land by the Indians, and had
not yet returned at the time of the United States Surveyor General's inquiry. The United States patent for over 655,000 acres exceeds the
eleven league maximum. See: Private Land Claims, pp. 868-875.

T. **TOWN OF MORA GRANT**
(D-68, pp. 180-192)

This is a town grant of the Mexican period (1835). Seventy-six persons were placed in possession of what amounted to two town sites: Santa Gertrudes (sic), 200 x 150 varas (yards); and San Antonio, 150 x 2,000 varas (yards). In addition, for crops, 4,100 square varas and 1,700 square varas were distributed at Santa Gertrudes; while at San Antonio 2,800 varas of land in the valley, 560 varas at the Lagunita, and 250 varas of land opposite the town, towards the southwest thereof, were distributed. The rest was for common pasture, or right of commons.

278

Donald C. Cutter, Ph. D.
Professor of Southwestern History
University of New Mexico
Albuquerque, New Mexico

I. ARTICLES

Bancroft, Hubert Howe, _California Pastoral_ (1769-1848),
San Francisco (1888)

Brayer, Herbert O., _William Blackmore_: _The Spanish-Mexican
Land Grants of New Mexico and Colorado 1863-1878_,
Denver (1949)

Brayer, Herbert O., _The University of New Mexico Bulletin_,
"Pueblo Indian Land Grants of the 'Rio Arajo'
New Mexico" (1939)

Caughey, John Walton, _California_, New Jersey (1940)

Espinosa, Gilberto, "New Mexico Land Grants," _The State
Bar of New Mexico 1962 Journal_

Hafen, LeRoy R. and Rister, Carl Coke, _Western America_,
Englewood Cliffs, New Jersey

Keleher, William A., _Maxwell Land Grant_, New Mexico

Keleher, William A., _Law of the New Mexico Land Grant_,
New Mexico (1929)

279

Morrow, William W., _Spanish and Mexican Private Land Grants_,
San Francisco (1923)

Servin, Manuel P., _The Act of Sovereignty in the Age of
Discovery_

Torchiana, H. A. van Coenen, _Mission of Santa Cruz_, San
Francisco (1933)

U.S. Department of Interior, _Federal Indian Law_, (Rev.
Ed. 1958)

II. STATUTES AND DECREES

1 Stat. 50, Northwest Ordinance of 13 July 1787

Recopilacion de Leyes de los Reynos de las Indias

Plan of Iguala, 24 February 1821 (Pronouncement of Agustin Iturbide)

Treaty of Cordoba

Treaty of Guadalupe-Hidalgo, 9 Stat. at large 922

Mexican Colonization Laws of 1824 and 1828

Senate Executive Document 49, 48 Cong., 1st Sess. (U.S. Govt. Docs. Serial 2162)

Rockwell, A Compilation of Spanish and Mexican Law in Relation to Mines, and Titles to Real Estate, Vol. I, New York (1851)

Documents Relating to Private Land Claims in New Mexico, 3 Vols., (pertinent portions also contained in Defendant's Exhs. D-67 through D-80)

III. CASES

Chouteau v. Molony, 16 How. 203 (1853)

Johnson and Graham's Lessee v. McIntosh, 8 Wheat. 543 (1823)

United States v. Maxwell Land Grant Co., 121 U.S. 325 (   )

United States v. Moreno, 1 Wall, 400 (   )